About the Author

Author "Dash" uses this as his pen name. He was born to Dr Dharampal Deswal and Mrs Sukhdevi Malik Deswal in a village called 'Ladhot', district Rohtak, state Haryana, in India. After his schooling in his native village and then in the city of Rohtak, Jhajjar, he went on to his college to study marine engineering in Calcutta. He is a regular seaman. He is a marine chief Engineer, as well as an examiner of engineers and an auditor. He is a published author of a book called *Ankahi the Untold*, and is a poet too. He is well-versed both in Hindi and English writing, and draws his inspiration from Paulo Coelho and Ayn Rand. He has had a long career at sea, for more than twenty-six years. He prefers writing stark truth and believes in the freedom of literary creativity.

Queen Corona Coronation

Dash

Queen Corona Coronation

Olympia Publishers
London

www.olympiapublishers.com
OLYMPIA PAPERBACK EDITION

A CIP catalogue record for this title is
available from the British Library.

ISBN: 978-1-80439-647-6

First Published in 2024

Olympia Publishers
Tallis House
2 Tallis Street
London
EC4Y 0AB

Printed in Great Britain

Dedication

Dedicated to my father, the late Dr Dharampal Deswal. My Guru and a man of infinite wisdom.

Acknowledgements

This book is a result of persuasion from my wife, Dr Vageshwari Deswal. She believes in me. Heartfelt gratitude to the men who sailed with me. To my chief Engineer, Parvinder Singh, and the coffee that he made for me. To all my neighbours, who always encouraged me to share my views. To 'The Iron Lady' of our house, my mother, Mrs Sukhdevi Malik Deswal, and my loving brother, Sudhir, and his family. To my kids: Varalika, who is now pursuing her Master's in Law at King's College London, and my prodigal son, Vinirjai Singh Deswal. Thanks to all the seas, rivers, and ships who let me be what I am. I acknowledge the patience and good work of my editors and proof readers from the office of Mr Parimal. I do acknowledge sincerely, Olympia Publishers for considering my work for publication. I have strived to put in my efforts to bring events from news, social media, and from social gatherings. A tribute to all the doctors, paramedics, social activists, governments, scientists, and ordinary men who fought against COVID. May humanity win always.

Preface

This book will take you through the various dates of chapters, where you find a daily account of the years 2019, 2020, 2021, and 2022. The remains of 2019 pass on to 2020. And the deadly coronavirus strikes.

I have written as and when my mood permitted me to write. The book is written at various cities, seas rivers airports. As I travelled even during Covid days. There are continuous details of my days as they passed, and at times breaks of months, as I froze along with my pen and time. I have tried to write in a way so that this book can be preserved for future generations. To read about corona, the passing of Queen Elizabeth, Coronation of King Charles, and how years changed.

This book is the result of my personal views and my readings. As I am not a doctor, the reading is based on my literary views only. But it will certainly give a good insight into COVID-19. Its birth, its manifestation, and its acceptance and cure in the end.

One who likes to read true events that happen daily might cherish reading this book.

Day 1

25 March 2020, Wednesday

Today, on 25th March 2020, I sit on my balcony of flat number 202, of Tower 3, projects Emaar Palm Gardens, Sector 83, in Gurugram (a city known as Gurgaon before), State Haryana, India. Yesterday, at eight p.m., Prime Minister Mr Narender Modi addressed the nation through all the television channels. And he broke the news to the nation that all will have to stay indoors at home for the next twenty-one days, till 14th April 2020, midnight. The dreadful and deadly disease of coronavirus, known as COVID-19, broke out in China's Wuhan province in October or November 2019.

It then steadily marched on to other countries, first through travellers, and then strangely even in people who made no contact with first patients. The Prime Minister addressed the nation earlier, too, just a few days back. After which, a "Janta curfew" or, you may say, a public self-imposed curfew was put into place, which indeed was a high success. By now, Italy was devastated, with about six thousand deaths. The mighty USA has a staggering death toll of thousands. Europe is engulfed in corona, and so is the whole world.

So now it's decided by the Indian government too, to clamp down, lock down past the extent of curfew, a scenario when none will be allowed outdoors. None, that is. India is a diverse and overly populated country of 1.25 billion people. It is at high risk.

The labourers who had come to make a living in big cities now head back to their respective hometowns, which aggravated the risk of transmission and now a complete curfew was enforced in Pan India. Let me tell you the scene which has unfolded thus far. A team of doctors in SMS Hospital Jaipur treated three patients, all above sixty-five, and cured them. They said they have used a combination of drugs, Copravir, and chloroquine. They were the first to declare such a cure from India. Then there is Dr Sushila Kataria, a well-known physician at Hospital Medanta Gurugram, who, with her team, cured eleven Italian patients in about twenty days of time. In her interview, she advised not to worry, but to isolate oneself. She told there are symptoms like flu, and it is only a type of viral flu, which when diagnosed and treated early is totally curable. She said only ten per cent of patients would need admission to a hospital, and healthy people who take caution and medical help can get rid of this coronavirus disease. The above situation for the elderly population is grim, as told by a minister from Israel on television. He suggested total segregation of the elderly from the younger population. Death in Italy is predominantly of elders only. A country with Europe's most aging population, and one of the best medical facilities in the world.

President Trump tried to bring a big aid package but was blocked by opposition there. Yesterday, Mr Modi announced a fifteen thousand crore package to fight corona in India, which would be used in procuring ventilators and beds, and training paramedics. Worlds face a challenge collectively of unprecedented cooperation. The disease has put this generation, who is watching fearfully from their isolation in homes, through the net and TV, Newspapers. Palm Gardens, is society where I live. Actually, the people nowadays had stated to stay indoors

14

and be cautious at least a week ago. Though, we went to our cousin's destination wedding by train to Naukuchiatal, near Nainital in Uttarakhand, but that was about ten days back. A tab is kept on all the bride and groom's side guests, all in total about a hundred and fifty. The bride's family travelled from the US, UAE, and other countries. Luckily, all left for their respective places and, so far, all are keeping healthy. But I believe it was a huge risk. But fifteen days back, the situation was totally different than it is now.

Now, already, a positive case has been detected in the same building, Tower 3, Flat No. 902: Mr Rohit Sharma, who returned from London, along with his wife, but the wife is negative luckily. Mr Sharma is admitted to Fortis Hospital and is faring well. I hope he comes back safe. Now, the scene is that a greater number of travellers from abroad were suspects initially. But it has spread in the local populace too. Today, cases in Haryana: thirty-one total, twenty active and eleven recovered, all treated by Dr Sushila and her team. I will not go into numbers that much now. It's like a scoreboard, with a neck-to-neck fight between Maharashtra and Kerala. Total cases in India: six hundred and twelve, at evening six p.m. Italy's new cases now dropping. China seems to be coming back to normal. The rest of the world is still fighting it out. Pakistan, UAE, Saudi, SA, and India doubled in the number of cases between fifteen and twenty-one days. The corona menace is the level playing field. It's treating rich and poor alike. There is news of Prince Charles, seventy-one years old, heir apparent to the throne. Queen Elizabeth, nearing one hundred, is safe. Charles, unluckily always, I guess, is at the receiving end. I will mention hoaxes, conspiracy theories, and facts before I go to sleep. And then I will continue tomorrow. Numbers of newer cases are slowly and steadily rising in India.

It floats on social media that the coronavirus came from bat soup in China. Similarly, SARS, another epidemic a few years back, was from birds, also called avian flu. There was swine flu from pigs, and MERS, another respiratory tract infection flu. There is talk of the hantavirus now, from rodents. Interestingly, all major recent outbreaks at least had a mention of a link with animals. And nowadays there is a go-vegetarian trend emerging. A go-vegan trend is also abuzz in Europe. A scientist talked about the erstwhile pandemic like the 1918 Spanish flu, and how it got transmitted all around the world. He says it's airborne and due to new technologies emerging, especially interference in aerial space. Now, he links corona with 5G testing and releases in internet services.

Day 2

26 March 2020, Thursday

I had slept after writing last night. Dreams have taken on a disturbing pattern thanks to the fear of this disease, in the form of monkeys and insects attacking people. Now, on the morning of 26th March, yesterday there was talk about food and water for stray dogs. People, a few good people, are still feeding them by wearing masks and sanitizing themselves. There is no news now the world over, except news of COVID-19 or coronavirus. Coming to speculations, some say it's a leak from a bio lab in Wuhan, China, which was testing bioweapons.

The Italian mass spread is also blamed on the "Hug a Chinese" Campaign by the mayor of an Italian town. A lot of Chinese people, under leader Xi Jinping, have started to spread Chinese businesses and culture all across the globe. Bergamo in Italy and Wuhan in China had below twenty degrees Celsius. Nobody knows if the high temperature will kill this virus. Bergamo and Wuhan bore the brunt of this deadly disease. An audio clip is circulating on WhatsApp, the single largest source of news and socializing nowadays, ahead of Facebook and Instagram, all under the ownership of Mark Zuckerburg. So, this audio clip now says its source is a Chinese friend of the Indian voice in the clip. It says that the virus stays in the throat for three to four days and forms a glue-like liquid with sputum. This chokes the lungs as it goes down. He suggests having lots of hot water every day, and pass this virus to the gut, where gastric juices dissolve and neuter it. Then it is safely passed out as excreta. The scene with people is paranoid, fearful, restless, and rumor-mongering. Streets, roads, shopping malls, even housing societies all wear a barren look, free from people. The only places with activity are hospitals. Indians are keeping their fingers crossed and obeying the lockdown. The sufferers are daily labourers, street hawkers, shopkeepers, private security agencies, guards, transporters, and practically all. The stock exchange in Mumbai has kept dropping steadily, but no one is even thinking of investments. People are praying to stay alive with their families. Phone calls have increased instead of messages on mobile phones.

The birds are more audible and visible. There is literally no noise pollution or air pollution. The air pollution index in Gurugram is in the eighties, where it had once gone to six hundred.

The governments world over are giving parole to prisoners and releasing some. Fear and the spread of corona seem like fair game, as nature is getting revived. Men who spoiled it are in lockdowns as a punishment. Dolphins were seen in Venice waters; after God-forsaken years, it happened. The US has passed a two trillion dollar bill for aid to the corona fight.

The bill has gone to the House of Representatives. Spain and Italy are the worst hit, with above seven hundred deaths daily. Italy's death toll is seven thousand five hundred plus now. France is another country to be hit en masse. Now, South Korea has released an app that tracks the history of travel for people. Almost all of the national and international air spaces are now seeing no traffic movement. Nigeria witnessed the mass looting of shops. Italy's dead are burned in isolation and the country has run out of burial caskets. Cases in the US are seventy thousand now, with a thousand dead already. China, now having almost recovered from its cases, is now focusing on becoming a champion in helping other affected countries like Italy. Trump calls it a "Chinese Virus", and China mocks the USA for not handling it properly and unnecessarily blaming China. China seems to have enough resources now. People now wear masks and gloves and carry sanitizers. No one touches anything directly, be it elevators, cars, gates, or switches, in common areas. "Namaste", the Indian version of saying 'hello', is popular now the world over.

Day 2 (Continued)

26th March 2020, Thursday

The only vendor of milk and vegetables in society has refused to come today. Security in the society of Palm Gardens, Sector 83, Gurgaon, complains of guards being removed, and all not being paid by agents or owners. We sneak a walk with our pets, a male Lhasa Apso "Astro" and a female mix of Lhasa & Shih tzu "Maya." Often in garb for getting essentials, we go out to shop in society, and when no one is in the vicinity, we remove masks and breathe some fresh air. Fear of other people barking back at you is as much as that of corona. My wife feels claustrophobic and is restless being locked at home.

I have never written so much in a single day as nowadays. I watch Vikings, two to three series, and a movie or two a day. I do not have earphones, so I am the only one mostly watching TV or shows aloud. The rest are all hooked on to their devices with earphones.

I sit for long hours on the balcony. I see two to three houses near open fields, a few strays, and some birds. The gardener of a society gone a few days ago. Now, the grass is growing, and the hedge, too. In fifteen days, it will wear a wilder look. I am looking forward to seeing that. It did rain in the last two days.

I grew up on Hollywood movies and English novels. More often, I read of World War I and II and epidemics and famine outbreaks in the world in fiction, or in movies and novels based on real stories. But here, we are witnessing fear, as well as liberation in a way. Thoughts of material possession are dim now and living amid enjoying the gift of life is more. Strangely, politics is so supreme, most people in India and elsewhere criticize or appreciate government gestures depending on which side they are on, even in these times. There are fights (virtual) on FB and WhatsApp groups for and against the government. Numbers thus far have risen to around a hundred new cases or below so far in India. Some seem to rise to million, as no testing is done here in large numbers. I see it as maybe there are no symptoms in people in that big number as in Spain, Iran, USA or Italy. Strangely, my mind goes to colder temperatures there and it being only a variant of the flu. I hope numbers will dwindle and die down in the hotter months coming now, at least in India and the hemisphere. Then again, I could be wrong too, no one knows. By now, at six p.m., seven hundred and sixteen cases in India, twelve deaths, and forty-two recovered. The media is functioning so far.

I wonder, in today's world, if we had no media, how would people connect, with no news, no socializing, nothing, especially for people below thirty-five years or so, who had already seen the era before the cell phones. Anyway, they are handy in lockdown. Remarkable chirps or birds are now audible, and loud. It's soothing. The positives of a lockdown, nature might revive a bit.

Day 3

27 March 2020, Friday

Now, the mornings start by checking out a link app which counts the number of new cases, recovered, and dead states-wise and nationwide, updating live. Sad, a morning that augurs with bad news from all around all day. People keenly observe the progress of the disease in their countries, states, cities, localities, and housing societies they are living in. The worst that I feel is each looks at the other like he or she might be infected and hiding. Or he or she might not be doing enough on their part. The full-blown symptoms surface after ten days or so, that is what is said. I write on the basis of social media news. People suggest having lots of warm water, garlic, ginger, green tea, and hot air above fifty-five and fifty-six degrees Celsius, which kills the virus, and on and on. Safest probably is to stay isolated for long periods, as the virus dies down its natural death.

Today, China is back on partially. The USA has the greatest number of cases. Italy has the greatest number of deaths. India probably testing the least in proportion. Pakistan not doing enough at all. A group of G20 nations announced five trillion dollars for the fight against COVID-19. A Nobel prize winner, Michael Levitt, a Nobel prize winner in Chemistry at Stanford University. It appreciates social distancing in the USA, and predicts better results than China or South Korea, and foresees a quicker recovery than thought. Meanwhile, there is social media gossip that Australia shall be locked down for six months. News from Italy is few now, but the dance of death continues there. India today by morning has seven hundred and thirty-five cases, fifty recovered and sixteen deceased as per COVID19india.org, an app that I use to track situations in India. Kerala and Maharashtra continue to top the list, a list each doesn't want to be in.

Relatives and families are now segregated, each staying where they were at beginning of the lockdown. The migratory labourers are now trying to board trucks and reach home. But they are rounded up and locked up, wherever they are caught. There are scenes of people going to offer Namaz in mosques, flouting the lockdown, and are also beaten up by police. Now the biggest question is, could there be humongous numbers in India if tested more?

I, with my understanding, say numbers add simply to panic. About eighty per cent of infected patients don't require hospitalization. And only one per cent would need intensive care. Time only will tell which country's approach was best.

It's been raining for the last three days now, bringing temperatures down, which no one wishes. The scene in rural Haryana is: all staying indoors, whole villagers getting sanitized. Villagers are on the social vigil, blocking entries and exits to the villages. The tradition of smoking hookah and playing cards is being stopped. People smoke hookah alone now, not socially. Leaders like Deepender Hooda, Abhay Chautala, and others have come out to donate to the relief fund.

It is a lovely drizzle while I am penning down, but my mind is weary. Around six p.m. today again. For the first time, the count in India shot above one hundred and fifteen new cases today. The count is now above eight hundred and fifty confirmed cases, seven hundred and fifty-nine active, seventy-three recovered and nineteen no more.

By now, Spain has overtaken Italy's death toll in a single day. About eight hundred people died in a single day in Spain. The count of dead is nearing five thousand now. Cases seem to have spread to the slums of Mumbai. The daily toll is mounting in Maharashtra and Kerala now. Politics stays as politics is expected to be. Now, President Bolsonaro of Brazil has bowed down to evangelical church priests and churches will remain open in lockdown in Brazil. With large support from this section, Mr Bolsonaro was elected. Pakistan tried to bring about the topic of J & K in the SAARC meeting hosted by Mr Modi. They are pathetic politicians, even in such times.

Numbers have gone past eight hundred and sixty-three by the time it's seven p.m. now in India. Prime Minister Boris Johnson tested positive, after Prince Charles in the UK. No one is above coronavirus spread. Before I end the day's writing, let me share John Hopkins University research. Though I got the same only as a forward on WhatsApp, nevertheless I share again for everyone's viewing. Which goes as:

The viral infection of COVID-19 has to do with RNA Sequencing. Seasonal flu is an "All human virus." The DNA / RNA chains of the virus are known to human response in form of immunity. Before it comes around each time, at times at the specific time of year. It's either by exposure or by flu shots you get immunity. But novel viruses come from animals. The WHO tracks novel viruses in animals; usually only animal-to-animal transfers happen. But once these animal viruses mutate and transfer from animal to human, the human immune response doesn't recognize it. So, we can't fight it off. Once the infected human virus mutates, it now spreads from human to human too.

Now it produces a new contagion. Depending on the fusion of this new mutation, it decides how it will spread or how deadly it's going be. H1N1 was deadly, but it did not mutate in a way that was Spanish flu. Its RNA was slower to mutate, and it attacked its host differently too."

Now about the ongoing coronavirus. It existed in animals only, but it made a jump in December 2019, in an animal market, and transferred to humans for the first time. In Wuhan, China, it had mutated in animals and jumped to humans, but within two weeks it mutated, and human-to-human transfers happened. Scientists call this quick mutation "slippery".

Since humans had no immunity to it, it took off like a rocket. And there are no known medicines, either. It causes great damage to the human lungs. This one is slippery and that's why it is different from H1N1 or other types of influenza (Flu). Now it has two strains. Strain "S" and strain "L." This is a lung eater virus, more deadly because of two strains difficult to make vaccines too (twice as hard).

In the historical context of flu infection, those who stayed isolated survived, like Henry VIII, who never met anyone till the Black Plague passed. And he survived.

Day 4

28th March 2020, Saturday

Good day to all. Here I sit down again, not writing any happy tales of these days. Italy lost nine hundred and nineteen men & women again in a single day. But also, a good bit of news is that nine hundred and twenty-five were recovered there. Nine hundred and nineteen in maximum deaths so far reported in twenty-four hrs. The USA's number of infected is one hundred and four thousand, now the maximum anywhere in one country. Countries like Jordan and Brunei are reporting the first cases or first death at the moment. We have two pets, as I told you earlier. We take them for a walk; that's the only leisure left. A quick five to ten minutes, with faces wrapped in masks. We clean their paws when back with sanitizer. And yes, we sanitize too. The number of cases in India at eleven a.m. is nine hundred and two total, of which eight hundred are active, eighty-three recovered and nineteen deceased. It has become a count of numbers on a minute basis all over the world. Trump announces one hundred thousand beds with ventilators in quick-time manufacturing. India lacks a lot in that. India is on prayers. The mass explosion of stage three looms large now, as per the news, in the next week; let's see. But as I follow, we might not have that big number due to the lockdown in place in the early stages. You never know that Ayurvedic and other home remedies might be preventing or safeguarding. But it is all left to guess.

Six forty-five p.m.: numbers in India have risen to nine hundred and forty-five so far, but eighty-three have been cured and gone to their homes. Cuba is sending a huge number of doctors and medics to Italy. A country of communists who now boasts of good health care. Trump has evoked Defence Act provisions and asked GM (General Motors) to make ventilators. Opposition is cursing President Bolsonaro for not being strict and letting churches be open. Bolsonaro goes on to say some people will die, but the whole thing is blown out of proportion. Meanwhile, here, near Palm Gardens, in my society, in nearby slums, the government is distributing rations and free masks. The elected MLA Mr Rakesh Daultabadji is doing his bit privately as well. He is a good Samaritan. The isolation does induce anxiety in minds here, but one needs to fight it off, with movies and series on Netflix or Amazon Prime or other serials. Today, "Ramayana", a series of the eighties, is started again for people. It's auspicious Navratri too, where Hindus worship Goddess for nine days and fast. I heard a temple bell toll today after many days. It sounded more concerned than anything else about why people are still out in open.

I formed a small NGO by the name EK Haryana, about four years back. It is coming in handy to send out positive messages, for the same member went out in markets and marked round circles with chalk or lime three meters apart. A way to enforce social distancing. We are in the middle of creating a corona relief fund too, which is initiated. Another NGO member donated cash to the slum, and another food for the homeless. There is a talk of the pandemic might be for six months, so grow vegetables in pots in the backyard in the society garden

A one-hundred-and-two-year-old Italian grandma has beaten corona at this age; she gives confidence to the elderly

27

population for survival. She was possibly infected with the 1918 Spanish flu too. Doctors are taking samples of her body to study. Doctor Sicbaldi treated her and named her 'Immortal'. The doctor says she was very positive, and the doctors did little. She was born in 1917.

Day 5

29 March 2020, Sunday

This is no different morning, and this is no different scene, except a few of the maids who stopped to come to work. After waiting a few days, they had come to collect their dues. Guards are excited at the welcome sight and have surrounded them for chats. Maids also giggle and flirt back. Now a few fatsos' overweight mistresses have arrived with cash in hand, to give to fitter women. The scene all around is nothing moving at all.

The positive outcome of the lockdown is a drop in pollution levels. In Delhi, it has dropped to twenty-five, almost similar to that of Bhutan (a carbon-negative country). After many days, a lawn mower was whirring in the lawns of society. The sound was uplifting. Numbers except that in China are rising. Everywhere of dead and newer cases. In India, it stands as one thousand and thirty-seven confirmed cases: nine hundred and twenty-seven active, eighty-five recovered and twenty-five deceased. Italy's death toll has gone past ten thousand. The USA's hotspots of infection are on the rise, Detroit becoming the new epicentre. In Nigeria, police used tear gas and batons to disperse mobs. My wife and I sneaked a walk past ten p.m. in silence around unoccupied towers. We are always scared. We let off masks when no one is in sight and breathe deep, gulping of fresh air. In horrified minds, we walk and climb stairs, the moment a person is in sight we move away to an entire new walk path. An accidental touch to the railing is devastating in mind. We don't touch the face at all, already ninety per cent covered high with masks. Sanitized hands too. Any items coming from outside are first dumped in the wash basin and washed with soap and used after an hour or more. The fear of uncertainty doesn't leave any moment. What will be next?

So far, there has been no let-up in Europe, especially in Italy and Spain. Princess Maria Teresa of Spain is the first royal life claimed for death by corona; these coronated royals are also not spared corona. She was the cousin of King Felipe of Spain. Prince Charles remains steadily moderate fighting corona off. India's disastrous migration of labourers continues, and it is debated in the political circle for and against. But for sure this rampant migration needs to halt, and people need to be stationed wherever they are to minimize the risk of COVID-19 transmission.

A man who was quarantined in Sri Lanka returns to Tamil Nādu in India, but only as a madman. He bites a woman to death. The quarantine and the total isolation are also doing bad as they are doing good. Now, it breaks morale and makes laymen, an ordinary man, believe something drastic dangerous is about to happen. It surely crushes freedom. There is a big talk among intellects about whether religion is worth practicing or not. I think many will shun religious practices if not religion totally, as an aftermath of corona.

In my neighbourhood: now I have a count of visible souls, five horses, two strays, five pets on leashes with four owners including me and my wife. About six security guards, a random gardener, two to three people in balconies, no kids, and a single elderly gent who is at times without a mask. He comes to the main gate and returns. He dresses up well. Today, in a nearby field, visible from my balcony, the mustard-ready crop was harvested by four labourers. Few signs of life around make me happy and pray for their safety too. Now, there is news that a German finance minister, fifty-four-year-old Mr Thomas Schafer has committed suicide; in wake of the corona crisis, he feared economic fallout. His death is a surprise to his German citizens and a shock to the world. In India, too, cases have increased to one thousand one hundred and twenty-seven so far by eleven-thirty p.m. Delhi shot up by twenty-three cases in Kerala, and Maharashtra is still at the top, with numbers rising in Karnataka too. There has come news of one Dr Vladimir Zalalea, who has successfully treated sixty-nine COVID-19 patients in NY. He uses Hydroxy-chloroquine-sulphate, zinc, and Z- Pak with a hundred per cent success rate. He says the whole treatment costs twenty dollars and five days only. The breathlessness, he says, is cured within four to six hours.

Day 6

30 March 2020, Monday

I want to start writing on an optimistic note today. Dr Peter Gotzsche, MD, founder of the Cochrane Collaboration, has published more than seventy-five papers in the BMJ, Lancet, Annals of Internal Medicine, and New England Journal of Medicine. Here is what he says: "Almost everyone I talk to, lay people and colleagues (I am a specialist in internal medicine and have worked for two years at a department of infectious diseases, I consider the pandemic of coronavirus a pandemic of panic, more than anything else."

Another doctor in France: Dr Didier Raoult, MD, Ph.D. His credentials before his statement are worth knowing: Director of the Research Unit in Infectious & Tropical Emergent Diseases. Professor of Infectious diseases faculty of Medicine of AIX-Marseille, University.

-Classified among the ten leading French researchers by the journal Nature.

-Has over two thousand scientific publications.

-Has discovered ninety new bacteria.

-First to discover large-sized viruses.

Here is what he says: "Actually, of all respiratory infections, it's probably the easiest to treat. So, there is really no reason to get excited any more. There is really no reason to get excited and rush to produce a vaccine."

Another gentleman, Professor Pietro Vernessa, MD.

-Chief physician of Infectious Disease, St, Gallen, Cantonal Hospital.

-Found that around eighty-five Y (eighty-two to ninety per cent) of all infections occurred without anyone noticing the infection.

He believes: "Based on the new insight, we also have to understand that many of the measures that we have implemented so massively today may even be counterproductive".

Now, here is Prof. Yoram Lass, former Health Ministry chief of Israel.

- Former associate dean of the Tel Aviv University of Medical School.

He says that the new coronavirus is "less dangerous than the flu" and lockdown measures "will kill more people than the virus." He adds that "they do not match the panic", and psychology is prevailing over science. He also notes that "Italy is known for its enormous morbidity in respiratory problem, more than three times any other European country".

Dr Frank Ulrich Montgomery, president of the German Medical Association, president of the World Doctors Federation, argues that lockdown measures as in Italy are "unreasonable" and counterproductive, and should be reversed.

He feels it's a measure of political despair only and not of reasoning.

Dr Wolfgang Wodarg.

-MD German pulmonologist.

-Former chairman of the parliamentary assembly of the Council of Europe.

-In 2009, he called for an inquiry into alleged conflicts of interest surrounding the EU response to the swine flu pandemic.

He feels the politician is being coveted by scientists, scientists who swim along in the mainstream and just want to be part of it.

What is missing now is the rational way of looking at things. He says, this needs to be asked, "how did you find it dangerous, is it something new?"

Dr Sucharit Bhakdi, MD, microbiologist.

-Former head of Institute of Medical, Microbiology and Hygiene, one of the most cited research projects by scientists in Germany.

He says in length that "The government's anti-COVID-19 measures are grotesque. The life expectancy of a million is shortened. The horrifying impact on the world economy is threatening the existence of millions. Already, services to the person in need are reduced. Operations cancelled. Hospital personnel dwindling. This will impact profoundly our society. All the measures are leading to self-distraction and collective suicide based on nothing but a spook".

Lastly, I would quote Joel Kettner, MD, professor of Community Health Sciences and Surgery at Manitoba University.

-Former chief public health officer to Manitoba province.

-Medical director of the International Centre for Infectious disease.

He says, "I have never seen anything like this anywhere like this. I am not talking about the pandemic, because I have seen thirty of them, one every year. It is called Influenza, and other respiratory illness viruses. We don't always know what they are, But I have never seen this reaction and I am trying to understand why?"

A friend contradicts the view of these notable gents of

science and medicine. He says, in view of few men against the entire WHO, it leaves a layman in persisting limbo. The cases in India are now one thousand two hundred and sixty-three confirmed cases, one thousand one hundred and twenty-seven active, one hundred and four recovered, and thirty-two deceased. The scene in my society: the only infected person, Rohit Sharma, has come back cured in nine days. The security guards and a few residents clapped when he made an entry back. I clapped too, and shared news with other groups, as it raises hope. In New Delhi, a seminar of Muslims was held in Jama Masjid. Muslim scholars from Malaysian society attended and a huge mass of Indian Muslims congregated too. Now it is feared that two hundred might be affected. One or two of the attendees are feared dead already of corona. No confirmed news gets as to how many. And unprecedented unity is seen in many Indian and world citizens too. But worldwide, seven hundred and twenty-three thousand, seven hundred and thirty-two cases and thirty-four thousand deaths from the COVID-19 virus outbreak. Wuhan shrimp seller, Wei Guixian, is argued to be the first corona patient, a disease which has mauled the entire earth by now. Severely stretched health facilities are relying on field hospitals now, mostly roping in their armies, police, paramilitary forces. India has readied railway wagons and coaches. The Army and Airforce are making field hospitals, five of them. Each county is gearing up for massive outbreaks. The talk of the economy getting hit is upbeat. India is already making task forces to fight on two fronts, the corona health care, and economic care too. Israeli Prince Minister will go into quarantine as his close aide tested positive.

There is news of European governments rejecting Chinese healthcare products. The war after corona will certainly be on economic lines. The total number of confirmed cases in Italy rose to ninety-seven thousand, six hundred and eighty-nine from ninety-two thousand, four hundred and seventy-two, but the lowest daily rise. Yet seven hundred and fifty-six more Italians were lost to corona. Spain reports eight hundred new deaths and Iran one hundred and seventeen new deaths. The Tokyo Olympic games are to take place in July 2021 now. It is still better news than scrapping their game altogether. Libya has freed four hundred and fifty prisoners in wake of this crisis. But Belgians all are hit with numbers in thousands. Russia is relatively spared, with one hundred and eighty-three cases and deaths. They still mull over options to lock down the entirety of Russia. Iran's death toll is two thousand seven hundred and fifty-seven. Spain after Italy has passed China in the number of deaths by now. India plans to keep its twenty-one days lockdown to 14th April only and not beyond.

Day 7

31 March 2020, Tuesday

I had a couple of sneezes yesterday, enough to play havoc in my mind in the current scenario. I immediately took Matrix LC as medicine. I normally take it against the cold that makes me sleepy for twenty-four hours, but I had to. The situation remains as it is for India, USA, Italy, Spain, Iran, Europe, and Asia as it was twenty-four hours before. Italy extends their lockdown to another few days to 2nd April. The USA are gearing up for a longer lockdown than others. The only recreation available is phone and T.V. The case of the Nizamuddin Muslim gathering has got twenty-five positive cases. A man who attended the same from the Philippines is reportedly dead. Delhi government is keeping an eye. It is believed that they were one thousand five hundred people, who also perhaps offered Namaz at Jama Masjid.

I forgot to mention I am a seafarer; I am a marine engineer and a chief engineer of fifteen years. A superintendent engineer, and also an examiner of engineers to the Mercantile Marine department of India. I am giving my introduction to my mariner's fraternity and others, as I am narrating stories of sailors and families in times of corona.

Sailors basically are the least talked about people in society. Their heroics have never been noticed and never sung. They silently ferry cargo to and from one end of the world to another via ships and sea routes, crossing rivers, seas, and mighty oceans.

Even now, while I am penning this down, a ship somewhere in the Atlantic, somewhere in the Pacific, the Indian Ocean is quickly whaling our needed goods. Our food, clothes, steel, oil, oil products, gas for industries, fuel for cars, and almost everything we need. One of my fellow seafarer's wife visited a psychiatrist yesterday. She broke down, staying alone with a small girl and frail elderly in-laws. She cooks and looks after the house and them. Her husband, a chief officer in Merchant Navy, was due to arrive in January and suddenly this crisis lockdown, now he is stuck on board for an indefinite period. God knows when his reliever will go to relieve him. This housewife, the wife of his, was waiting for a few months for his arrival. Now she is sitting in front of a psychiatrist and sobbing, worried about what will happen. Likewise, there are so many stranded-on ships unable to come home. Brave seafarers were ready to relieve them ashore, but now cannot, due to bloody corona.

While I am writing, flashes of my own call of duty move in front of my eye. In tough times, doctors, medics, and politicians will all be praised, but never the sailors. Someone once told me they are cursed and sent to seas. Damned be this virus, and ridden be the world of it. Like sailors, all other professionals working abroad are stuck: students, IT professionals, engineers, contractors, and other professionals. May all be safe and reach homes once lockdown and flight restrictions are lifted.

At six p.m., the number of confirmed cases in India is now one thousand four hundred and forty-two: one thousand two hundred and fifty-five active, one hundred and forty recovered and forty-seven deceased. There is politics taking centre stage in the US and China: the blame game is on. The US plans to shift two hundred of its manufacturing to India. China is now seen by the world as a villain who unleashed, knowingly or unknowingly, the virus COVID-19 on the world. There is a message on social media advocating Chinese masks, mechanically made by machines, over handmade, unhygienic Indian masks. World Bank warns of an unprecedented shock to the world economy and probably only India and China not going into recession.

The global infection has reached eight hundred thousand. US sixteen thousand five hundred, Italy one hundred and two thousand, Spain around eighty-eight thousand. Death toll is around thirty-seven thousand eight hundred. Now, after Italy and Spain, the US death toll has surpassed China's. Interestingly, all are developed economies and leaders in health services. A field hospital is being set up in New York's iconic Central Park. China's Wuhan, the problems starter, reports no new case now in a week. It's almost ten days now here in Emaar Palm Gardens, Sector-83, Gurugram, with no activities, and no people in sight barring a few, who are seen as violators of the lockdown. It's sickening to live under house arrest. My friend, the first female marine engineer in India, has the same thoughts as mine.

A persisting fear of corona, even with a slight cough, fever, running nose, or sore throat. We have altered sleep patterns. And also, the burden of domestic work too. It's evening, rather pitch-dark night; it is, by now, about ten p.m. Rain has fallen again now, giving a break of a day. Since all factories, all cars, practically everything is shut, the voices of birds in nests, crickets cricketing and dogs barking are far heard. These are firsts for city dwellers. The air quality is so excellent, the skies are clear blue in the day, and now the stars twinkle, as if animals are hailing these times. I wish this virus dies, never comes, and these cleaner days stay forever.

I wish humans learn to respect nature and learn to live in symbiosis with all. Maybe we are meant to be vegetarians, and unnecessary animal eating has released this, out of animals to human viral infection, maybe. Sadly, in the real-time world now today, so numbers have risen to their maximum in a single day for India: one thousand six hundred and fourteen confirmed, one thousand four hundred and nineteen active, one hundred and forty-eight cured, forty-seven deceased. All keep checking the numbers daily, the curves, the graphs depicting the state of the infection across the world and also locally. Good news from Italy: new cases saw a steep fall, but Italy lost above eight hundred again in the last twenty-four hrs.

Day 8

1 April 2020, Wednesday

It's morning again in the locked-down house. The scene is the same as was for the last almost fifteen days now. People started living indoors before Modi's official declaration to lock India down. I roll my eye in each direction from my balcony, north, east, west, and south all bearing the same look, the empty roads, and only a few security guards at the post. No movement at all. A few cars left society gates, maybe to fetch essentials from only a single market that is left open nearby in Sapphire Mall, under police protection. Guys are sanitizing society once again. They are wearing gloves and masks, no eye covers, and backpacks of sanitizer liquid-filled tanks. They pump manuals and guide the hose to spray around in mist form.

World-over, the situation seems to be different in different countries. Ireland confirms their cases have halved. The UK shows signs of flattening the curve. This is a sign of things are under control and maybe recoveries have new cases. Sierra Leone confirmed their first case. In Holland, one thousand have already died, with a total infection of twelve thousand five hundred and ninety-five.

Markets have crashed the world over. Crude prices went up to one thousand one hundred and twenty-two dollars. Global deaths have passed forty thousand. One hundred and seventy-four thousand and nineteen people have recovered, too, and eight hundred and twenty-three thousand four hundred and seventy-nine remain infectious. Italy, China, America, and Spain have more than one hundred thousand cases. Still, people are locked inside houses, and police use tear gas, beatings, and bleach.

In India, it's a fight on two fronts; the hungry daily labourers daily vendors, small shopkeepers, errand runners, and part-timers. And the infected patients. Indians are showing great resolve and unity; the well-to-do are donating. All big business houses – Reliance, Tatas, Mahindra, Infosys, Wipro, and Baba Ramdev's Patanjali – all are donating to the PM relief fund for corona, and NGOs are working to send packets of rations; some are feeding daily. Camps are set up for transferring houses and shelter for the needy. A few good Samaritans in Rohtak, my hometown, have let their hotels be used as shelters and makeshift hospitals.

I had written about Muslim Congregation in Delhi. It stands corrected as a "Tabhlighi Zamaat" in Markaz Masjid. The meetings or gatherings happened in the Mosque located in the Nizamuddin area of Delhi. The "Tabhlighi Zamaat" means adopting, promoting, and going back to the prophet Muhammad's days in terms of dressing, living, and practicing Islam. So, this meeting in times of corona has left more than thirty-five positive cases or suspected cases. Turkmenistan has forbidden the word "coronavirus" and also forbids people to wear masks; it could be a religious reason.

But certainly, the virus is impartial to all. There is a new rumor now that since Indians have "BCG" vaccinations, they are less susceptible to coronavirus. I say a rumor it is. And there is this bunch of young Indian engineers with a start-up named NOCCA Robotics busy building low-cost ventilators for Indians which should cost fifty thousand Rs or one thousand five hundred dollars approximately. They have three prototypes ready already. A group of seven engineers plan to be in the market by 7th April, right now tested for prosthetic lung. Saudi has urged Muslims to postpone Hajj booking. Death keeps soaring in Spain, despite a slower new cases rate. UN says corona is the biggest threat since WWII. New cases emerge with loss of smell and taste said to be symptoms of corona.

Day 9

2 April 2020, Thursday

The new thing that has set in is irritation. Most friends have become quarrelsome, with almost no tolerance levels. The quarantine has started to hit people's minds. After nine days, I left my building premises to get vegetables, and the scene in town is appalling and grim. There were about a thousand people scattered in small groups on the roads. Passer-by cars stop to give them food packets and there is almost like a stampede; neither the benevolent donors nor receivers at their mercy were wearing masks. And of course, no social distancing either in shops or near cars on road. Then came a car speeding; the middle-aged guy on his phone signaled the nubile beggar girl to hop in the back seat. And he sped away.

Prostitution and beggars are encouraged. These beggars do not contend with a day's meal or today's ration packet. They are hoarding and begging for more. I see a collapse of lockdown and it's at most downsides today. Yesterday was the single highest rise in case cases in twenty-four hours in India. The figure by now is two thousand and ninety-four confirmed cases; one thousand eight hundred and sixty-six active, one hundred and seventy-one recovered, fifty-seven deceased. It has spread pan India and is disastrously high in Kerala and Maharashtra. In the world, by now fatal infection is nearing a million marks. Last week saw a double of cases. For the last few months, except for news of corona, there is no other news. All sports business, political, and religious social activities have ceased. I definitely see looting and crime next if India extends the lockdown.

Returning to the notorious case of "Tablighi Zamaat" in Markaj Masjid, Nizamuddin, Delhi. Now it is no longer a secret that foreign Muslims from over one hundred countries had assembled in Markaj, Nizamuddin. Many who managed to return homes have died of corona. After the disposal from Delhi, many went to their respective states, like six positives in Telangana, and likewise in Tamil Nādu and other states never tested positive. I did see a video recording where a senior gent, an elderly Muslim scholar says that corona has occurred due to people not going to mosques. The video does show scores of Muslims leaving different rooms that all had to be asked to vacate. No force was used in it. There were cases shown on television where health workers in Muslim colonies were chased away and pelted with stones. Even if corona doesn't spread in India or in Muslims (which in fact has already been detected as a positive case in Indian Muslims too) it still is a violation of the Government's orders not to assemble in large numbers and all had been urged to remain indoors. Now, visas of some foreign Muslims are held up and they are arrested. A FIR has been filed. Famous Indian security advisor Ajit Doval had to reach Markaj in person at night at two a.m. and intervened in getting those areas vacated. For the last three days, a big chunk of coronavirus cases are spread out due to this "Tabhlighi Zamaat" held in Markaj, Delhi. The cases now in India at six p.m. stand at two thousand one hundred and ninety-six confirmed, one thousand nine hundred and fifty-four active, one hundred and seventy-six recovered, and sixty-six deceased. The count in Haryana has risen to forty-nine confirmed, twenty-two under treatment, twenty-seven recovered

45

and no deaths so far. After the fallout of corona, Shanghai becomes a Chinese city to ban eating cats and dogs. The world will embrace vegetarianism more after corona, an animal-to-human viral infection, generated from the Wuhan animal meat market.

Scientists in Australia have begun testing two potential coronavirus vaccines in "milestone trials." There are several other vaccine developments on in the world, including Indian Companies in it. A human trial was done on two volunteers in the USA, a male and a female, a month ago. Now, an Aussie lab is testing the same on animals. It was, in fact, four patients' recoveries at Kaiser Permanente research facility in Seattle. The first person to receive was forty-three-year-old female, Jennifer Hallow, in Seattle. Spain's death toll is past ten thousand now, with two hundred and fifty deaths yesterday. Some governments are trying or have already used absolute powers in the garb of corona spread. The latest is the Cambodian government.

Iran's total cases have reached fifty thousand four hundred and sixty-eight, with three thousand one hundred and thirty-six deaths. UN Secretary-General says that post recovering from coronavirus, the world will be a better place. Just while I am writing, I checked again on the site COVID19 India.org, which now reads as two thousand three hundred and seventy-two confirmed, two thousand one hundred and twenty-seven active, one hundred and seventy recovered and sixty-six deceased. It has become a game of numbers that suddenly shoot up.

Day 10

3rd April 2020, Friday

Yesterday was mayhem, with Tabhlighi Zamaat participants getting tested positive in hordes. Fanatic sections continuously believe in "This being wrath of Allah in nonbelievers". Rampant spitting and sneezing videos to spread corona were seen on social media. If they are to be real, which it appears by seeing, then maybe humanity has not seen hatred in earlier times. Health workers are being chased and pelted with stones by Muslims. Spitting on cops and so on. The fallout is hundreds who attended Markaj getting tested positive. This Tabhlighi Zamaat is banned by many Muslim nations too.

They have had a tiff with police and security forces in Pakistan, too. Visas of attendees of this Zamaat in Nizamuddin are cancelled and blacklisted. Even wiser Muslims have condemned their illiterate acts by some. The whole faith of Islam is tainted by such practitioners. But never blame the entire faith or religion on a few. Islam is a religion of peace. I hope religious scholars of Islam guide these people back to fall in the line of peace and goodness and have faith in science too. Figures in the morning read as two thousand five hundred and sixty-seven infected, two thousand three hundred and three active, one hundred and ninety-two recovered, seventy-two deceased. Mr Modi released a video message for all at 0900 hrs today, which asked all to light up candles on 05th April to show solidarity as one nation together against corona. This is a sort of morale booster too. As apprehended, he didn't mention an increase in lockdown, which was dreaded thought. I hope construction activity revives and factories open too after the 15th. The global death toll is past fifty thousand and cases past a million. US Theodore Roosevelt's captain asked for help, as they got infected. A ship with a four thousand-strong crew. It's a US ship. The situation remains the same in Spain, Italy, France, the UK, Iran, the US, and elsewhere. Indonesia is seeing the most deaths after China in Asia.

Captain Brett Crozier, the captain of Theodore Roosevelt who raised the alarm, has been removed. He had said that the Navy is not doing enough to halt a coronavirus outbreak onboard the aircraft carrier. And the Philippine President says won't tolerate lockdown violations – "Shoot them dead!" President Rodrigo Duterte has warned firmly. The idea is less to single out Muslims here but to single out violators and spreaders of this menacing disease, be it from any faith. These are Hindus and Christians who violate in form of, for example, partying on Bondi Beach, or marriage ceremonies that I know are organised by Hindus in NCR Delhi.

I had a long conversation with a Muslim friend, a neighbour. He stressed, in fact, the Muslim faith emphasises a lot on personal hygiene. Cleanliness is half of faith; wash hands before and after meals, wash hands after going to the toilet, wash hands and feet daily, each of the five times before prayers, take baths before the main weekly prayers on Fridays. Also, rituals of bathing the dead before burial. Well, whatsoever it takes, we must win over this disease, else we are crippled from normal life for a long time.

Coming to why I am doing it: why am I writing almost like

a daily or hourly report? Because I, a forty-six-year-old, have never seen anything remotely close to it. Not in movies or books. I have heard the 1918 flu pandemic passed on without creating mass hysteria, as the media and medium of transmitting news was much less developed than now, where news reaches each living human. When such microanalysis is available to each naïve reader or viewer, it is bound to cause hysteria. Even world wars must have affected only warring nations and allies, only on borders mostly. This corona, through media, has shaken each soul around.

And it is changing each moment for the worse so far. At times, there appears no end in sight or in near future. This complete resumption of international flights and normalcy of lives without masks looks like a dream. When will ever people hug in real without fear? And now rubber bullets are fired at South Africans defying coronavirus orders. Putin from Russia has sent a military plane to the US with supplies to fight the virus.

The notoriously secretive Gurbanguly Berdimuhamedov, Turkmen president and "father protector" since 2007, is dealing with the pandemic by essentially believing/ pretending that word coronavirus is banned from usage. Elsewhere in the world: in Ecuador, dead bodies are piling up. In Italy, the worst hit, there are so many dead bodies that forklifts are used to lift coffins and loaded into military vehicles for mass burials.

On 12 January, less than three months ago, the coronavirus was confined to China only. But by 13 January, the virus became a global problem. Cases were reported from South Korea, Japan, and Thailand. Soon the US followed. And slowly the numbers swelled across the globe, and it turned into a pandemic. There are few islands who have not reported a single case and even some landlocked countries too.

So far, eighteen countries are spared the wrath of corona. Comoros, Kimbati, Lesotho, Marshall Islands, Micronesia, Nauru, North Korea, Palau, Samoa, Sao Tome, and Principe, Solomon Islands, South Sudan, Tajikistan, Tonga, Turkmenistan, Tuvalu, Vanuatu, Yemen. Out which, a few, like the war-ravaged Yemen and dictator-led North Korea, for example, might not be reporting. The night is at peak and midnight. The day for India has not gone well, with a rise of five hundred and sixty-three cases in a single day, the biggest and the first five hundred plus cases. The total now is three thousand one hundred and eight confirmed, two thousand seven hundred and ninety-three active, two hundred and twenty-nine recovered, and eighty-six deceased. The deadly virus onslaught goes on a killing spree and rampage across Europe, the US, and half of the world is locked down. There doesn't seem to be any respite or let-up cases or any new methodology or vaccine or drug to cure it so far. People have become zombies, continuously staying locked indoors in fear and by force of government both. I feel if it goes on like this for another month it could devastate unthinkably.

DAY 11

4 April 2020, Saturday

Now, two things are impacting everyone, everywhere: the fear of the unknown and the fear of uncertainty. My thoughts are fixed on the calamity, day and night, like everyone else's. Sleep patterns are distorted, and I do get disturbing dreams. Mostly reflections of the day's sad news all the time.

Prime Minister Modi has appealed yesterday to light candles at nine p.m. for nine minutes on 5th April night. This is probably a collective prayer against corona. The scene from my balcony has been exactly the same for the last twelve to thirteen days. No people in sight except plants, a few birds, one or two gardeners, and a few security men at the gate. Residents don't come out nowadays, not even on their balconies, and this is strange. A rare glimpse of change in sight is welcome. A piece of news was shared by some friends that they have been asked to resign or accept lower salaries. The ill effects of corona and lockdown is visible all around the globe. People losing their jobs. Lawlessness could be next, if this scene goes on for months. The labour class who works daily to earn, to feed themselves, are rendered jobless. How long will government and social organisations feed them? I think not very long. The labour in India is mostly from Bihar UP, MP Rajasthan, West Bengal Orrisa, Chhattisgarh, and Jharkhand, most of whom have returned back to their native places.

The remaining, I presume, are stuck due to the lockdown and the day it opens all will leave. The real lockdown of factory construction and other activities which are labour-dependent will then happen. Cases of domestic violence against women have risen, as per news from NCW, the National Council for Women in India. The worst hit is women working from home with no maids and minimum support from children and spouses. They work, as domestic servants, as wives, as mothers, and as employees all at the same time. The poor labour clan of women is in danger of being exploited sexually for money and food.

The talk going on in all of India is of "Markaj", the mosque of Nizamuddin, Delhi, where Tabhlighi Zamaat had happened. And the talk with facts and videographed evidence is that sixty-five per cent fresh increment in total cases is because of infection spread by attendees of Jamaat. So much so that it has spread to fourteen states. In Delhi itself, two hundred and fifty-nine cases of a total of three hundred and ninety-two from "Jamaat" attendees. On Friday, people tried to go to the mosques, flaying orders of lockdown. When police intervened, they were charged and pelted on by stones. A similar scene was recorded in Pakistan, which then opened mosques to people. The people from Markaj who tested positive were admitted to hospitals, where some died midway. There were cases of violence, spitting, and nudity by their men.

Now, UP Government has put them under NSA, National Security Act. They will be punished. A lot of rumor-spreading Tik Tok and WhatsApp videos surfaced, "provoking Muslims to refrain from a social distance, as hugging and eating from each other's plates spreads love as per Islam." Not many learned Muslims came forward to teach these mostly teens and young men. But police have registered cases and the majority of them have been arrested. It is sickening to see doctors being attacked and people evading treatment and tests.

Referring here to a UN statement which had warned of the severity of the increase in cases in the Gulf, I hope people wisen up to this clear movement and presume danger. I hope innocent men are not framed by the government and only culprits get punished. Coronavirus has impacted EU unity and almost all have firmly sealed their borders. Care homes, where the mostly elderly European population were living, have borne the brunt of the virus attack most. Thousands died sad, lonely deaths, without any near and dear ones, and many without any last rites. Many Christian men were buried or incinerated. China is now on the brink of the total coming out of corona, mourning its dead from the epidemic and saluting its people who fought against it. Russia is planning to use software with facial recognition via CCTV cameras to identify coronavirus cases. It is debated in Russia for its efficacy. New cases slow down in Italy and Spain. The US is going high continuously and so is the UK. The US saw one thousand deaths in the last twenty-four hours.

Trump is arguing against the use of masks. That is a strange thing. Masks are the first solid barrier against coughing and sneezing in some people, and there are thousands of untested roaming around. Well, that's America then. Trump also fired the official who triggered impeachment in his Ukraine intelligence case. I am just writing this to show that corona also serves as an opportunity for politicians to decimate the opposition. Some claim it is an emergency and use emergency power to stay in longer than tenures. The cases in India at six p.m. are: three thousand four hundred and seventy-four confirmed, three thousand one hundred and forty-five active, two hundred and thirty-eight recovered, ninety-one deceased. Almost all states show a jump in numbers, some increased by the Markaj effect too. Northeastern states show minimum or no numbers at all; that's a good sign.

Midnight, and there is nothing positive to narrate once again. I watched a movie just to unwind and take my mind off the perpetual news. The USA lost one thousand four hundred and eighty people to corona in a single day.

The ripples of Markaj continue, increasing numbers in India too. Now the question looms: for a country of one hundred and twenty-five crores, are enough tests done? Do we have enough facilities? Or are we actually less affected than colder Europe or Russia or USA? Time will tell. Pakistan is in dilemma, whether to save people from hunger or from corona. They are taking a mid-path, cautious approach. The religious fanatics hit Pakistani authorities in laying curfew harder than India. I feel equally bad for my brother and sisters stuck there in almost a depleted economy and now this. I hope the world emerges a better place post-coronavirus elimination.

Day 12

5 April 2020, Sunday

It begins from where it was left yesterday. And it has been the way life unfolding for almost a month. The unrelenting coronavirus keeps spreading and keeps killing people all around. There is almost no positive news from any corner, be it the development of a vaccine or a new effective drug. The line of treatment for this viral infection is differently done by different nations. In Thailand, the red-light district of Pattaya, Bangkok, and others have been shut down. Clubs and massage parlours are closed, and beaches are closed. Tourists blocked. That has left about three hundred thousand sex workers out of jobs, pressing some into venturing into lonely streets at odd hours, prompting crime and vulnerability of at least one of them. Nicaragua, Burundi, Belarus, and Tajikistan have not barred their football league and the sport is still in action there. The USA is facing accusations of outbidding Euro nations and procuring the bulk of masks for themselves alone.

There was this doctor, Dr Ai Fen, who was the first to find out about one of the earliest patients, a patient with flu-like symptoms. She tried treatment with the normal treatment available, but failed when she conducted the same tests which revealed the SARS virus. She started sharing her findings. First one to respond was Dr Lee. Now Dr Ai Fen is missing, adding suspicion to the way coronavirus was handled by Chinese authorities.

I am letting in any information that trickles to me to pass on as it is to readers. The whole writing might not be as well-strewn as a beginning-to-end story with a fixed situation. It is a real-life story that has never been witnessed seen or written earlier. It has overwhelmed one and all. The most powerful of nations hit hardest, the USA, and developed countries next. So far, poorer and developing nations are considered lesser priority, only after developed countries are dealt with first.Is it less testing or otherwise? Time will tell. A doctor friend from London says, "It will not survive harsh summer high temperatures like May in India."

A vaccine seems a year to a year and a half away, maybe coming from Germany or the UK. My Indian bioscience research scientist, Dr Arshad, feels it might be India giving the solution to the world in a year's time. At five-thirty p.m., the confirmed cases in India total three thousand eight hundred and nineteen, three thousand four hundred and seventeen active, two hundred and ninety-five recovered, one hundred and seven deceased. The Markaj runaways have now shown up in numbers as patients. This is a typical example of the failure of social distancing and if it could not have happened, numbers would be lower here. The government has confirmed the cases have doubled up in the last four days, clearly due to Zamaat cases spreading it.

People have started to lose jobs now. Air Deccan ceases all operations, all employees put on 'sabbatical without pay'. ICMR, Indian Council of Medical Research, says there is no evidence of COVID-19 being airborne yet. Relief campuses and shelters have been put up all across India. NGOs, individuals, and governments are setting up these help centres. Testing capacity in India has been ramped up to ten thousand cases per day. In Haryana, more than thirty cases were directly added by "Tabhlighi Zamaat" itself. The pandemic world-over has claimed more than sixty thousand lives so far. Nearly three-quarters of these are in Europe alone.

Pakistan has two thousand seven hundred cases now, Britain forty-two thousand, and Spain's deaths are eleven thousand seven hundred and forty-four, overtaking all. The previous flu pandemic of 1918 was known as the "Spanish Flu". Singapore has eleven thousand one hundred and fourteen cases total, of which one thousand and twenty-three COVID-19 positive cases are linked to Jamaat, reported from seventeen states' health ministries on 5th April. Now, let's dig a bit into the line of treatment going on around the world. There is currently no vaccine against COVID-19; it is a viral infection and not a bacterial one. If your symptoms are more severe, supportive treatment may be given by doctors at home or at a hospital, which may involve fluids to reduce the risk of dehydration and medicine to lower body temperature or fever. Oxygen support is given in more severe cases. People who have a hard time breathing on their own may need a respirator. Some medicines are being tried and tested and investigated for protection against SARS-CoV-2 and treatment of COVID-19 symptoms.

(1) Remdesivir is a multi-spectrum drug for viral infection, used on Ebola. Treatment is not yet approved in humans. Two trials were done on someone in China and another by FDS in the US.

(2) Chloroquine has been in use for over seventy years and has been effective for malaria and autoimmune diseases. Researchers have found that it is effective against SARS-CoV-2 virus in studies done in test tubes. At least ten clinical trials are ongoing.

(3) Lopinavir and Ritonavir are sold under the name Kaletra and are designed to treat HIV. In South Korea, a fifty-four-year-old man was treated with a combination of fluid drugs and had a significant reduction in his levels of coronavirus. WHO recognizes Kaletra, in combination with other drugs, could be beneficial.

(4) APN01. Scientists developed it in 2000 and found a certain ACE2 protein is involved in SARS infection. This protein also helped protect the lungs from injury due to respiratory distress. COVID-19, also like SARS, uses the ACE2 protein to infect cells in humans. Trials are ongoing for its larger and more effective use.

(5) Favilavir. China has approved the usage of the same against COVID-19. The drug was initially developed to treat inflammation of the nose and throat. It has shown efficiency in actual use, on seventy patients.

Day 13

Good day to all. I am not going straight to the numbers of dead or infected. I want to begin with some positive news thus far on COVID-19. Australian scientists tested an anti-parasitic drug, which killed SARS-CoV-2 Virus growing in cell culture within forty-eight hours in lab settings. Ivermectin is an FDA-approved anti-parasitic drug, which has proven efficiency against HIV, dengue, influenza, and Zika virus. Research published in a Journal of Monash University showed that a single dose of Ivermectin could stop the growth of coronavirus in cell culture, effectively eradicating all genetic material of the virus within two days. Lead author Dr Kylie Wag Staff has said even twenty-four hours shows a significant reduction in viral RNA.

Dr Wag Staff, however, cautioned that tests were in-vitro and needed to be carried out on people. Dr Wag Staff had a previous breakthrough on Ivermectin in 2012, where she, along with Professor David Johns of Monash University, had highlighted its anti-viral properties. They started research soon after the SARS breakout. Some believe that the spread of COVID-19 is already there in a much larger number than tested. If it is so widespread, there are fewer deaths by ratio and it might prove herd immunity already happening. More and more countries are containing it. Lockdowns are effective too. For example, Singapore and Taiwan were able to tackle this thanks to their SARS 2002 experience of theirs.

Researchers have a head start, as SARS-CoV-2 pathogen is similar to coronavirus. Clinical trials of the potential vaccine are ongoing in China, testing methods to stimulate our immune system. The first US clinical trials for a potential vaccine have begun in Seattle. The biotech company Moderna has taken a piece of genetic code for a pathogen's protein – the part that's present in other viruses like SARS – and fused it with fatty nanoparticles which can be injected into the body. Imperial College London is designing a similar vaccine using coronavirus RNA, its genetic code. The Pennsylvania biotech company Inovio is generating strands of DNA and hopes it will stimulate the immune system.

Johnson & Johnson and French pharmaceutical giant Sanofi are both working with US Biomedical Advanced Research and Development Authority to develop vaccines. Sanofi's technique is to mix coronavirus DNA with genetic material from a harmless virus, while Johnson & Johnson will attempt to deactivate SARS-CoV-2 and switch off its ability to cause illness. Already existing anti-viral drugs such as REMDESIVIR and anti-flu drug FAVIPIRAVIR may have some effect on COVID-19. Almost every country is busy making new biomedical devices, such as ventilators, carrying stretchers and mobile testing units, and other devices specific to COVID-19 patients, where isolation is of importance.

Doctors in India have used a combination of drugs to tackle HIV, swine flu, and malaria and have been successful in curing them. And doctors from Japan and China have successfully transplanted the blood plasma of recovered patients into ailing patients, with good results.

I am back to check the current status of the COVID-19

spread, beginning with India. It's six p.m. Confirmed: four thousand five hundred and two. Active: four thousand and forty. Recovered: three hundred and thirty-seven. Deceased: one hundred and twenty-five. The world over has seen one million, two hundred and eighty-seven thousand, three hundred and eighty-one cases: seventy thousand five hundred and fifty-four deaths, two hundred and seventy-one thousand nine hundred and fifty recovered. Italy sees steady tolls: one hundred and twenty-eight thousand nine hundred and forty-eight cases, with fifteen thousand eight hundred and eighty-seven dead and twenty-one thousand eight hundred and fifteen recovered. In the USA: three hundred and thirty-six thousand nine hundred and six cases, nine thousand six hundred and twenty-four deaths and seventeen thousand nine hundred and seventy-seven recovered.

Spain: one hundred and thirty-five thousand and thirty-two cases, thirteen thousand and fifty-five deaths. Germany: one hundred thousand two hundred and thirty-two cases, one thousand five hundred and ninety-one deaths. France: ninety-two thousand eight hundred and thirty-nine cases, eight thousand and seventy-eight deaths. Iran has witnessed more than fifty thousand cases and around four thousand deaths. The story remains mostly the same. But I am hopeful that towards the end of this week, the virus will start moving towards the end in Italy, Spain, and Europe. It's our hope. The US might follow with good news next week. The severity appears less so far in south Asian and Asian countries, barring Iran and China. Let's see how it unfolds for the rest of the coming days.

Day 14

7 April 2020, Tuesday

UK Prime Minister Boris Johnson's symptoms have worsened, and he is moved to the intensive care unit. The "Tabhlighi Zamaat" attendees continue to torment India's efforts to fight COVID-19. Now, a fresh case of some of those under quarantine having openly defecated in Narela Quarantine Centre in Delhi. For God's sake, someone from the Islamic faith tells him not to spoil the faith's preaching, which believes that hygiene is half of the faith, while mankind attributes cleanliness to be a pleasing attribute. Islam insists on cleanliness.

Muslims are required to take care of their personal hygiene, by assuring that they are well-groomed, and their bodies, their clothing, and surroundings are clean. "Truly, God loves those who turn unto him in repentance and loves those who purify themselves." (Quran 2: 222)

Prophet Muhammad (PBUH) said, "the key to the prayer is cleanliness, its beginning is Takbir (saying Allah o Akbar) and its ending in Salam (Salutation; Abu Dawud). I will continue a little with what I gathered, though I am no Muslim, and no scholar, and not eligible to comment. But still, I urge my Muslim brethren, in their tough times of fight against COVID-19, that all should be reminded by Muslim scholars to:

Keep food and water covered, offer Salalah with a clean body and clothes, use fragrance or perfume, comb your hair, and use oil on the hair.

Take a bath and perform allusion for offering prayers. (in these emergency times, it can be done with restriction and as and when can be). Go to bed early, rise early, keep your house, and streets clean or, we can say, keep the environment clean. Keep your clothes and body clean, do miswak regularly (sources: plus point.ae) It's only a net search result, but I feel that not only Muslims, but all mankind should follow their beautiful teachings of Islam. This might aid in the fight against COVID-19 the world over.

The impact of the virus is seen to be lowering in South Korea, Italy, and Spain. I hope by Sunday we see a drastic drop in newer cases. The US and the UK might follow it; India might too within a month see the grip firmer and things in control.

The Ministry of Ayurveda or Ayush ministry has sent some guidelines for boosting immunity, which may aid in the fight against COVID-19. I keep sharing whatever information I keep getting and, of course, it's the readers' discretion and subject to verification, if one desires. But here are some tips for boosting immunity in Ayurveda. It also stresses that prevention is better than cure. While at the moment no vaccine or medicine is available. Ayurveda is the science of life. It propagates the gift of nature to mankind.

Ayurveda's extensive knowledge based on preventive care is derived from the concept of "Dinacharya" (daily regimes) and 'Ritucharya' (seasonal regimes) to maintain a healthy body and healthy life. It is a plant-based science. Ayurveda's classical, timeless scriptures are full of wisdom, prevention, and cures for diseases.

Recommended measures

(1) General measures

(i) Drink warm water throughout the day.

(ii) Daily practices of 'Yogasans' and Pranayam (controlled breathing exercises) meditation

(iii)   Take in spices like Haldi (turmeric), Jeera (cumin seeds), Dhania (coriander leaves), and Lahsun (garlic) in raw or cooking mediums.

(2) Ayurvedic immunity prompting measures.

(i) Take Chyavanprash (ten gm) 1 TSF in the morning. Diabetics take sugar-free Chyavanprash (Chyavanprash is a concoction of many herbs.)

(ii) Drink herbal tea/decoction/kadha, made from Tulsi (basil), Dalchini (cinnamon), Kali Mirch (black pepper), Sonth (dry ginger) and Munnakka (raisin) twice a day. Add jaggery or fresh lemon juice as per taste.

(iii)   Golden milk (half teaspoon of haldi (Turmeric) powder in 150 ml warm/ hot milk) once a day.

(3) Simple Ayurvedic procedure

(i) Nasal application: apply sesame, coconut oil, or ghee in both nostrils. "Prati marsh Nasya" in the morning and in the time of sleeping or evening.

(ii) Oil pulling therapy: take one teaspoon of sesame or coconut oil in the mouth. Do not drink, swish in mouth for two to three minutes and spit it out, followed by warm water rinse twice a day.

(4) During dry cough/sore throat

(i) Steam inhalation with fresh Pudina (mint) or Ajwain (caraway seeds) can be practiced once a day.

(ii) Lauang (clove powder) mixed with natural/sugar/ honey can be taken two to three times a day in case of cough or throat irritations.

(iii)   These measures treat normal dry cough and sore throat, however, it's best to consult a doctor on persisting illness.

It's midnight; a look at India and the world's condition. India: five thousand five hundred and thirty-seven confirmed, four thousand seven hundred and thirty-eight active, four hundred and forty-five recovered, one hundred and fifty-four deceased. World over: one million, four hundred and eight thousand four hundred and ninety-three total cases, eighty thousand nine hundred and forty-five deaths, three hundred thousand six hundred and one recovered, one million, twenty six thousand nine hundred and forty-seven active, out of which forty-seven thousand eight hundred and thirty-nine are critical. The US has become the biggest victim of coronavirus, with about one thousand three hundred deaths in past twenty-four hours. There have been no new deaths in China from corona. S. Korea has only fifty new cases. Italy & Spain's deaths have fallen, along with steady decline in new cases. India remains unpredictable.

Day 15

8 April 2020, Wednesday

I was again on Montair CC, a medicine that stops my relentless sneezing and irritation in the nose. So, it makes me sleepy. Today, the day has begun at six p.m. The mayhem continues unabated all around the world. India remains unclear, at least to me. I fear if we go the American way, we certainly don't have enough systems, especially doctors and other trained medics to attend to that large a number of patients. The Indian Government prior to this and this one too, in my opinion, lacks teeth to control private hospitals, which are the largest medical help at the moment.

In India, there are two types of medical facilities. One: those for the poor, which are shabby, unclean, and often run unprofessionally due to lack of resources. Two: private hospitals, like Fortis, Medanta, Wockhardt, etc. They have top-of-the-line facilities, but no room for poorer patients. Now, this government has begun "Ayushman Bharat", a programme to include the poor, too, into the ambit, catering free medical help up to five lakh rupees, about seven thousand eight hundred dollars. They have announced free testing and treatment of such poor patients now for COVID-19, too.

Yesterday, a meeting of all chief ministers of state and the prime minister was held. This mostly will lead to an extension of the twenty-one-day lockdown, which was supposed to end on the

66

14th at midnight, but will not be likely now. It may extend into May. Now there is the harvest season of crops in northern India, especially for wheat and other crops which were sowed in winter. Labour will be an issue. And social distancing will be impossible in it.

China has sprung a surprise; that they have a ready vaccine and same will be tested on humans soon and shared with the world in the coming months. China never fails to surprise.

It is very clear now that, pan India, the attendees of "Tabhlighi Zamaat", in Markaj, Nizamuddin Delhi, have spread into almost all corners. The truth is that almost fifty to sixty per cent of patients are Zamaat attendees. There are still people, like chief minister of West Bengal, Mamta Banerjee, for the sake of Muslim votes in her state, defending the heinous acts of spreading this disease by attendees on purpose, evading the law in unlawful gatherings in times of a lockdown, when attendees from scores of nations air travelled and congregated and later, went undercover to avoid being tested. When forcefully taken to the hospital, doctors and nurses were abused and attacked by them. Politics will kill more than the disease. A politician is a larger threat. And politicians from the ruling party victimizing Muslims for politics' sake is also condemnable. It is for all to understand that the virus does not spare or distinguish any.

Day 16

9 April, 2020

Yesterday, I was reading about the effect of medicine and slept through the day. So I couldn't write a few developments which I will include in today's writing. Yesterday was so far the worst day for my city, Gurugram; more than a dozen new cases were found and suspected death. There are stronger measures now and no spots are being marked and isolated totally; this is being done throughout India. There were fresh cases of misconduct from Markaj patients – they throw urine-filled bottles from windows in the streets. Why do they want to spread it? It is baffling. Why are some even refusing treatment?

In India, total cases this morning are now five thousand nine hundred and thirty-one: five thousand one hundred and eighty-six active, five hundred and sixty-five recovered, one hundred and eighty deceased. There were confusing and conflicting reports on the usage of the mask. One unverified WHO report said, "masks are to be worn only by patients and people involved in handling and treating them," and no one else, whereas some countries have made it compulsory to wear masks to go out in public.

Wuhan has opened up. There are no new deaths. Air space for international travel is already open, with extreme caution. Incoming international persons are screened many times and ones above thirty-seven degrees Celsius are not allowed to fly.

Once entering China, they are compulsorily quarantined for fourteen days, before the resumption of their duties.

The world's total cases are one million, six hundred and eighteen thousand seven hundred and seventy-three: eighty-eight thousand five hundred and five deaths and three hundred and thirty thousand five hundred and eighty-nine recovered.

USA: four hundred and thirty-five thousand one hundred and twenty-eight cases, fourteen thousand seven hundred and ninety-five deaths.

Spain: one hundred and forty-eight thousand two hundred and twenty cases, fourteen thousand seven hundred and ninety-two deaths.

Italy: one hundred and thirty-nine thousand four hundred and twenty-two cases, seventeen thousand six hundred and sixty-nine deaths.

Germany: one hundred and thirteen thousand two hundred and ninety-six cases, two thousand three hundred and forty-nine deaths.

France: one hundred and twelve thousand nine hundred and fifty cases, ten thousand eight hundred and sixty-nine deaths.

China: eighty-one thousand eight hundred and sixty-five cases, three thousand three hundred and thirty-five deaths. Iran: sixty-four thousand five hundred and eighty-six cases, three thousand nine hundred and ninety-three deaths.

UK: sixty thousand seven hundred and thirty-three cases, seven thousand and ninety-seven deaths. Turkey: thirty-eight thousand two hundred and twenty-six cases, eight hundred and twelve deaths.

India appears, by number, relevantly safe. But once community testing begins, the scenario may change. It might begin from Delhi soon, as Chief Minister Kejriwal has said on

TV. There seems to be a total curfew in Italy, as no latest updates are coming for the past few days.

Isolation is the best tool for countries to deal with COVID-19, so far. There is a race among scientists for producing the vaccine. The US, China, Germany, the UK, Israel, South Korea, and India could produce news in the coming two to three months. The spread is happening here in India, but luckily so far only in identified hot spots, which are contained and quarantined now.

The things that have developed in habits and psyche are everyone trying to eat healthily, sleep well and worry little. People are trying to get into good shape mentally and physically. A lot of old, dusty books are off shelves and into hands. More calls than texting. Junk foods are off menu. A simple sneeze creates havoc in the mind. Too cold items are not for now. The lockdown is certainly going to go to May or at least the end of April.

PM Boris Johnson of the UK continues to recover in ICU. The US is continuously hit, with about two thousand deaths in the last 24 hrs. Mass Ramadan events in Iran are put on hold or stopped. There is a prediction of poverty-stricken people dying of hunger in wake of the ongoing corona pandemic.

About sixty-six point six million Americans filed for unemployment last week and the total now is at an astonishing sixteen million mark. COVID-19 is and will change the world forever. Hopefully, survivors will see a better, less polluted, safe, and secure future.

Day 17

10 April 2020, Friday

The days and nights in total isolation, without work and without socializing, are wearing me down and my pen stops writing, it irritates me. I do not type on the computer. I write with a pen or pencil on paper. The daily mundane routine starts to get to you. Death and patients have become a game of numbers. At times, I tend to skip numbers and just read some positive news, if it is there. As per cases spread in my town of Gurugram, the society of Emaar Palm Gardens, Sector 83, Gurugram, is also put into a containment zone, which means that now police are at the gates twenty-four hours, and all absolute entries and exits are blocked.

Just now, while I am writing, a car approached the gate with a lady below forty and an elderly gent and a man in his forties. The man in his forties was driving and the woman sitting beside him. Now they are stopped at the gate by a policeman. I can see and hear the conversation. The man driving has cancer and is undergoing radiation therapy. The woman next to him is his wife. The elderly man in the back seat is the father of the patient. They are hassled and not allowed to get out too, without permission. They are waiting now. But long time, no permission for them.

There are others waiting to pick up their stuff from the gate. But no one was allowed to enter or exit. Men, women and kids are now literally under house arrest. Helpless people are peeping through windows or balconies.

In Italy, the last twenty-four hours brought bad news, as the number of deaths and new cases both rise. A country that is under lockdown since 9th March is anxious and on edge to come out of this hell hole. In the US, Dr Deborah concludes there are a greater number of male patients than female patients, though the number of families subjected to testing is higher.

Convalescent plasma therapy uses antibodies from the blood of cured patients to treat severely ill COVID-19 patients. Kerala is set to become the first state in India to do so. The health ministry in India denies community spread and says not to panic but take precautions. Spain saw the lowest number of deaths in the last seventeen days today. Italy is eyeing a lockdown extension to May 3. A professor in Milan who used to teach graphic design to a friend of mine, Rajesh Dahiya, told him that sleeping well and three good meals keep immunity good.

I keep sharing whatever my eyes or ear lay upon. Delhi Waqf board designated a graveyard for COVID-19 victims – "Jadeed Qabristaan" graveyard, near Millennium Park – for the last rites of COVID-19 victims of Delhi. The COVID-19 pandemic has sent the Indian economy to "severe demand shock" and it could "affect GDP, severely."

Pan India, now "hotspots" are identified and turned into containment zones and buffer zones around some. Unfortunately, I am myself "contained" in a containment zone now. Which means we cannot step out of our main doors. We keep immersed in watching TV and exercising gossiping. It might be a little tough on our two pets, who are used to relieving outside in the evening; talks are on with police to allow pet owners to take them out, maintaining social distancing.

Day 18

11 April 2020, Saturday

The mind wears out all, thinking clogs in chains. My pen stops abruptly, and I don't feel like writing mostly. That's how most of the day's writing stops. But I must muster courage and go on writing the facts, the rumors, the scenario, not only for readers of today but also of tomorrow. The flowers in my small flowerpots have blossomed, most for the first time. But it hardly recreates me. I want to go out. I want to hang out. I hope shaking a hand or a hug will not go out of fashion, post this. The scene is dismal. The lockdown which was to end two to three days from today, will now go on till 30th April, minimum.

I surely know, with resources available in the country and in ratio to the population and diversity of India, the lockdown will not go till a vaccine or till total disappearance of the virus. In hopeful news, there is a steady and sharp decline in new cases in South Africa. The death toll world over crossed one hundred thousand yesterday. The USA saw two thousand plus deaths. No one has a clear-cut strategy to deal with. China is seeing the second wave now, but in very small numbers. South Korea sees waning cases. Deaths are still happening at six hundred plus in Spain and Italy, but new cases are dropping. There was hope to see it better by today, but it has improved very little to rejoice.

If the virus remains and no vaccine or defined case, I am certain there will be riots, and people will break free from their homes. That might be a few months away. Never in my wildest dreams did I think that something like this would happen in my lifetime. But it is here already. The confirmed cases in India at eleven a.m. are at seven thousand six hundred and eighteen: six thousand five hundred and ninety-five active, seven hundred and seventy-four recovered, two hundred and forty-nine deceased.

A letter was shot to the commissioner requesting him to let the pets be taken for a walk. He was kind enough to allow a period of one hour in the day, with different slots for the dog owner. A single person with all safety measures, after being assessed for safety, will be allowed at a designated spot in society. My friend, Justice Parmar, was of the same opinion, that lockdown should be exercised daily but also humanely. My wife, Prof. Vageshwari Deswal, had taken this initiative here and got relief for all. At least relief for poor pets, who anyway have COVID-19 resistance so far.

The most moving and sad tales are patients dying of COVID-19 and not even getting last rites or meetings with near, dear ones in their last hours of life. Old age homes are out of bounds for Americans and many are not able to meet their parents or grandparents even during their sunset hours.

Spain has some pressure easing up as new cases fall straight for nineteen days now, and there is an announcement to open non-essential workers too, from Monday. WHO continuously warns about not opening the lockdown too soon.

Deaths in America have gone past eighteen thousand. In Italy and Spain, it's past sixteen thousand.

Meanwhile, my wife is shouting for joy in another room, as she learned the art of taking online classes. She was unable for some time. My teenage son, Vinirjan, had to be called in. I normally stay away from what I don't understand. Working from home and schooling at home is the new norm nowadays. And news from New York is that all the schools will stay closed throughout the year there.

There was news from Saudi Arabia; the virus has penetrated the inner sanctum of Saudi Royals, where one hundred and fifty royals are suspected to be positive. The king and prince have left for an island with important ministers for safety.

Day 19

12 April 2020, Sunday

It's a mockery of what's remaining of a Sunday now. All days are the same practically and so are all nights. Life in a containment zone is tougher than that in a lockdown state. There was frightful news to begin the day, with the reactivation of COVID-19 in patients in South Korea. So, for boasting of fast and strong measures, now there is this news that ninety-one patients who were declared cured have shown symptoms of Coronavirus again. Not of re-infection, but of reactivation of the same conditions of which they were declared cured. The scene in India has eight thousand seven hundred and thirty confirmed, seven thousand four hundred and fifty-three active, nine hundred and eighty-four recovered, and two hundred and ninety-three deceased.

The US now leads the world in coronavirus deaths, overtaking Italy. The picture is so grim. In Italy, one hundred priests, who come forward for last rites, have died of disease, and hundreds of medics, and policemen too, have died due to coronavirus.

It's Easter today and the march of the devil's own coronavirus is still on. People are celebrating online through calls and messages. Masses are cancelled. Leaders are posting messages to be hopeful. And hopeful one must be. Hope and positive determination are tools to fight it off for those infected and those trying to evade it. In the society I live in, there was only one active shopping mall, with all shops. That, too, is forced shut by the Government. The supplies of home deliveries are dwindling now and are not steady.

Ironically, the people enforcing lockdown, the police, the politicians, and the administration, all have access to the outside world and necessary supplies, but the ones forced indoors are not so lucky. There was an orator speaking in Arabic, shown on TV. He appeared to be a scholar. He was lecturing that the coronavirus is Allah's soldier to decimate the USA, and it will not affect Muslims. He is a Tunisian cleric, Bechir Ben Hassan, who lives in France, and has no doubt "the virus is a soldier Allah's army". It is toppling people in China as they had inflicted atrocities on Uyghur Muslims there. But sensible literate Muslims like one Mr Sameer Abbas in Delhi say, "that science must be respected, and bigger gatherings have caused spread of COVID-19, like one congregation in Markaj of Tabhlighi Zamaat" in reply to Tunisian cleric I mentioned above. An infuriated Ziyad Al-Handani, an internet user from Iraq, says, "don't try to take Allah's position. Allah doesn't burn wheat with the chaff, and Allah doesn't kill communities. If you are a true follower act like a human being."

The worst that is happening is people defying lockdown. Now in Punjab, the hand of a policeman was chopped off by hooligan loafers, who confronted the police party when asked to stay indoors. Another sad part is people doing politics even in these troubled times. Politics for votes, some appeasing and others condemning particular religious groups and linking whole community as troublemakers. The virus spares none. It just requires a host to foster upon, breed upon.

Meanwhile, in the UK, Mr Boris Johnson has returned back

to his residence recovered from corona.

I don't know if mankind has witnessed anything like this so far. It has been twenty days. I see the streets from my balcony, as I don't go out. And the scene remains the same, a few patches of green, a few palm trees, and narrow roads bereft of any humans. I look out a hundred times each day, day, day after day nothing changes. I wonder if it will end. If life will return to normalcy.

Day 20

13 April 2020, Monday

It's basically one has to wear oneself down completely. Exhaust totally by at least four to six hours of Netflix series or movies. Maybe a similar time or more on mobile phones, screens. About an hour's writing, some exercise, and repeat, day after day. Then you crash in bed by two a.m. of the next day and get up by nine a.m., pretending to sleep for an hour in the day. These are typical routines. PM Modi will address the nation again tomorrow at ten a.m. Most of PM Modi's national addresses are scary; they bring lockdown, change of currency, and such major issues. But tomorrow night brings some relief from locked-out routines, "locked in" rather on a small scale. Industries are expected to open. And some other non-essential services like construction etc. are expected to be announced 'open' tomorrow.

France, Spain, and Italy are seeing some respite in fewer deaths and fewer new cases. America is not so lucky yet. It's a battle of wits, sitting idle mostly at home and that, too, forced to be indoors. Whenever a delivery boy comes to the main gate, I already come to see him for a change. I had seen a lot of Hollywood movies, fiction, mystery, and aliens. I used to feel the way pandemics were shown in movies was only a movie thing. But it's worse, unimaginable.

There is absolutely no other news than that of COVID-19. There is no activity. As if the world is halted for some reconfiguration. Never before would earth and mankind have seen so many humans locked inside in homes in terror of a disease, that sometimes remain asymptomatic. There are so many theories floating around about the cause and cure of corona. And different nations are on different strategy paths to tackle it. From aggressive testing of South Korea to the ban on the utterance of the word "corona" by Turkmenistan.

I am not making any effort to stitch up a story here. I am writing it to be as natural as my mind is nowadays, decoherent and out of sync. It's not poetry, nor am I trying to make it rhyme. I am writing blunt, stark truth as far as possible, verifiable, and let it pass onto paper through my pen. There are about forty thousand seafarers stranded all around the world on ships. Uncertainty looms large over when they will get back to their homes. But, as usual, shipping is the least discussed topic, despite moving all the goods all around the world, much-needed medicines, ventilators, medical equipment, foodstuff and all.

By the end of the day, today ten thousand four hundred and fifty-three cases confirmed, eight thousand nine hundred and two active, one thousand one hundred and ninety-three recovered, three hundred and sixty-eight deceased. A fateful day with a maximum number of rises in a single day – one thousand two hundred and fifty cases added today. There are real people, somewhere far and nearby, getting infected and sheltering in the fight for life with uncertain treatment. Has it begun in India too? Is it inevitable to escape? Will all countries go Italy's way gradually? Time will tell. Italy's death toll passes twenty thousand. US Navy reported the first death of the USS Roosevelt crew, whose captain, Brett Crozier, was sacked recently for showing dissent about lack of proper care for the crew in corona times.

There is an increase in the containment zone now. Now, in pan India and in the world, the total cases are one million, nine hundred and nine thousand eight hundred and four: one hundred and eighteen thousand five hundred and five deaths and four hundred and forty thousand four hundred and thirty-nine recovered. So far, the graph has seen a rise, rise, and rise of new cases and deaths. The world now is fixed as to how to strike a balance between easing lockdown and containing the viruses. It appears May, too, shall be engulfed by this monster.

Day 21

14 April 2020, Tuesday

Prime Minister Modi addressed the nation today at ten a.m. on national television. As earlier declared, India's lockdown was to end today on 14th April, after twenty-one days. But it has now been further extended up to 3rd May. Testing has increased in India now and as a result, the number of new cases is increasing. For a reader who did not witness the horrible times of the coronavirus pandemic or who was in childhood and couldn't understand, the anecdotes written here might appear repetitive and boring. There were exact times, as day after day it was the same scenario, same news, same panic, same fears more each day; if you are looking to read a novel, it would almost be same story each page.

But this novel virus of corona left no wits untested, either of the nations, men in uniform, doctors, medics, housewives, and kids. Each was tested to limit, is still tested to limits to date. It's almost a month for some in India and abroad who have not stepped out of their houses. Doing nothing and living with a phobia of infection even from passing the wind, it's really a different and unprecedented situation for humans. It's midnight, and the day just passed. The number of confirmed cases was eleven thousand four hundred and eighty-seven, nine thousand seven hundred and thirty-five active, one thousand three hundred and fifty-nine recovered, three hundred and ninety-three deceased.

Isn't much change in India. The first twenty-one days of lockdown are over. Some stuck-up labourers are expected to be lifted. In Mumbai, Bandra, more than fifteen thousand turned up near a railway station in protest. They said they need food to eat and want to get back to their homes. The worst-hit city in India could not witness a worse scenario. God forbid, if only one was to be positive in that gathering, what havoc it would wreak. Italy is opening some shops, in Venice and elsewhere. Their condition appears better, with a steady drop in new cases and deaths. Though British PM Boris Johnson is out of danger from corona and is back home, the country still is in grave danger.

South Korea is shipping seven hundred and fifty thousand coronavirus test kits to the USA. IMF expects a meager three per cent growth for the world. The economies the world over getting hit are the most developed: UK, Germany, Italy, USA, etc. People the world over feel China's wrongdoing, in not letting out a warning to the world in time. And other conspiracy theories say that it is a lab-made virus. Interestingly, on 5 December, a major thing was seen when US and China signed a big trade pact. The unusual excerpts from the pact read, "a safeguard from God's act and pandemic". This is subject to verification. And interesting if found so.

The lockdown extends in India for another nineteen days. Interestingly in quarantine, the ships used to be laid up or made to wait for a forty-day period called quarantine. And India is doing the same now. Inmates in jails will probably suffer the most; already jailed, their visitation rights will be discontinued, and conditions inside jails are conducive to fostering viruses of any kind. May God help them as well.

Day 22

15 April 2020, Wednesday

President Trump of the USA first announced funding to WHO. He feels that three Chinese are to be blamed for this pandemic. Politics carries on with the ongoing plight of people. Trump adds his name to relief cheques worth one thousand two hundred dollars to seventy million Americans. This has slowed the delivery of distribution as, said the Indian PM, President, MP, and MLAs have declared a thirty per cent pay cut to be given as relief. Strict lockdown and quarantine measures are in place all around the globe. The bad impact of coronavirus could shrink the British economy by thirty-five per cent. Likewise, all world economies will suffer.

People the world over have also seen breaching quarantine in India, Africa, the USA, Europe, and practically everywhere. The countries are talking about lifting and easing lockdowns. There is an absolute lull in front of the coronavirus vaccine. No major breakthrough yet, only hope. In May, the pandemic will enter its sixth month. There is some hope for India to open up gradually after 20th April, as per new guidelines. But so far, new cases are increasing. The government says that despite numbers being above eleven thousand in India, there is no community spread. The temperature in Delhi and around are above forty degrees Celsius now. I hope it slows down its spread or kills it.

Indian scientists tested bats, and yes COVID-19 was

confirmed present in them. So, the theory of the origin of coronavirus, COVID-19, could be sure of connection with bats. People have gone nuts in lockdown amidst this COVID-19 scare. Some have pictures of their kid's head shaved off, with lady's fingers one end cropped at one end and planted on bald heads, giving it a similar shape to that of a coronavirus. Totally bonkers, another one, same thing but with a football and a kid charging at it, hitting it as the lady's fingers fly off and the mother shouts, "go corona go". I wish this virus would perish, else people will kill all with their incorrigible stupidity.

There was sudden good news of lifting the containment of my residential premises, the Emaar Palm Gardens in Sector 83, Gurugram. It brought joy and clapping from all residents from the balconies. It means now police will leave the premises, some gates might open, and a few walks can be started in the garb of night. Such are joys left now.

It brings sadness to me that men are hounded and rounded up like animals by police. Just a few ventured to grab a milk bottle or vegetables. Of course, some miscreants are always there. The first flight took off from Kerala to the UK to take a batch of two hundred and sixty-seven UK-bound tourists.

The whole game of quarantine did teach us a lot. Simple life, minimal stuff required to live, basically food and few clothes. Cars are lying parked in the parking for months now. The daily needs stuff of milk and groceries come from farm produce on daily basis. There is no need to hoard stuff. It encourages fresh stuff to be consumed. It is bringing the carbon footprint to "zero", as local produce suffices. A lot of activities, including education, can very well be done through the net and computers. No need to visit doctors for smaller ailments that can be cured on their own. Fresher, cleaner air prompts good health of humans and plants.

Day 23

16 April 2020, Thursday

If you are reading this daily update. So, by now you can compare the rise and rise of the coronavirus. And a rare victory in some control measures, containment may be China, South Korea, and the Indian, State of Kerala. An India District of Bhilwara in the State of Rajasthan also contained its spread of cases. In some rare good news, there is a small village in Italy where COVID-19, at the moment and so far, appears beaten. And except for some cases in South Korea, there have been no recurrences in cured patients. The theory establishes well in Wuhan's meat markets, from bats to pangolins, and pangolins to Humans, and then humans to humans. Before I go into the details of the day's happenings, I feel like recapping some new findings about coronavirus, the COVID-19. There is a huge division emerging now globally; it's like each for himself. EU nations are divided into relief efforts jointly. The US is backing off from giving aid to WHO. Nationalism flares in China, giving rise to xenophobia. Japan and Britain will extend their lockdowns. Why lockdowns? It's the simplest way to buy time, till sure shot detection, treatment and vaccines are available. Singapore, earlier praised for controlling the virus, sees a record rise in infection.

There was a debate on the use of ventilators by American doctors, some saying it is doing more harm than good. It's easier for citizens of a developed nation like the USA to file claims for jobs and livelihoods. But the poor and developing nations will struggle big time for providing salaries to non-working, non-contractual labourers, etc. India might face problems a lot. It's a problem, since we cannot open the lockdown, so daily earners cannot earn, and they cannot return to their villages, where at least they can thrive in agriculture or borrow from each other. The day has ended. We my wife and me stole a stroll with safeties or in an isolated patch in society.

In India: thirteen thousand four hundred and thirty confirmed cases, a rise of one thousand and fifty-nine cases today. Eleven thousand two hundred and fourteen are active, one thousand seven hundred sixty-eight recovered, and four hundred and forty-eight deceased. The world over: two million, one hundred and sixty-six thousand eight hundred and thirty-two total cases, one hundred and forty-four thousand five hundred and fifteen deaths, five hundred and forty-six thousand two hundred and sixty-nine recovered. USA: six hundred and sixty-nine thousand three hundred and seventy-eight cases, thirty-four thousand one hundred and three deaths. Spain: one hundred and eighty-two thousand eight hundred and sixteen cases, nineteen thousand one hundred and thirty deaths. Italy: one hundred and sixty-eight thousand nine hundred and forty-one total cases, twenty-two thousand one hundred and seventy deaths. France: one hundred and sixty-five thousand and twenty-seven total cases, seventeen thousand nine hundred and twenty deaths. Germany: one hundred and thirty-five thousand eight hundred and forty-three total cases, three thousand eight hundred and ninety deaths. UK: one hundred and three thousand and ninety-three total cases, thirteen thousand seven hundred and ninety-nine deaths. Till now, Europe has faced the wrath of COVID-19 most, then the USA and Asia. African countries are faring better. These were processions of cars and people, condemning lockdown in New York. Burmans said, "stop treating us like animals."

Day 24

17 April 2020, Friday

Days roll by; nights too. The judgment of killing COVID-19 goes on and on. People have accepted living indoors. There is hope India might open a little bit post-20th April. There were resentments shown by all the Europeans and Indians for lockdown, but most have graced this new but abnormal style. It's almost five months since it began in Wuhan China.

In India, for the last almost a week, about one thousand new cases add up, which is quite tolerable compared to what is happening in the USA. Delhi is showing signs of recovery, with less than one hundred new cases added now in the last three days.

My city, Gurugram, hasn't added a new case for the last four to five days. Russia has conveyed its thanks to the Indian government for the supply of medicines. India has supplied medicine to the USA, Russia, Israel, and many other countries in need. We have a good stock of chloroquine, hydroxychloroquine, and paracetamol, the main drugs used in this pandemic. Tabhlighi Zamaat's Faisalabad chief in Pakistan died of coronavirus. Maulana Shuaib's Rumi, sixty-nine, succumbed to the deadly infection of COVID-19. Muslim scholars need to educate the masses on this death-inflicting virus. Masses in mosques should be stopped temporarily. Foolish people targeting Muslims in the garb of this pandemic should also be punished.

But all faiths need to come together to fight this menace and respect social distancing, the biggest tool in this fight. Now there is news of people attending the temple chariot festival in Karna Village, in Karnataka's Kalburgi districts. Their religious fanatics should be criticized and dealt with as severely as any other violators. Post corona, I hope people believe in science more, their karma(deeds) more than blind faith. The world as a whole should respect Mother Nature more seriously than ever. There might be a drop in nonvegetarian eating habits post-corona. SARS, MERS, swine, hantavirus, historical rat plaques, etc. all originated from animals and got transmitted to humans. This might encourage veganism and vegetarianism more. There is a narration of all so far about coronavirus and COVID-19. As we know, the virus is from the family of viruses which caused SARS (Severe Acute Respiratory Syndrome), and MERS, which is Middle East Respiratory Syndrome. COVID-19 has been the most lethal, most contagious, and most feared of all pandemics causing contagion so far. This is described as a spiky ball of genetic material, coated in fatty chemicals, called lipids, and which sizes up to eighty billionths of a metre in diameter.

SARS-CoV–2 is the virus that causes COVID-19. It originated from bats and animals which would be in close proximity to humans, like pangolins, and then started spreading human to human, attacking their immune systems. It spreads by inhalation, and then it comes into contact with cells living in the throat and larynx. These will have a large number of receptors called Ace2 receptors on their surfaces (cell reception plays a key role in passing chemicals into cells). This virus has a surface protein that is primed to lock on that receptor and slip its RNA into the cell.

As per virologist Professor Jonathan Ball of Nottingham University, once inside, that RNA inserts itself into the cell-sown replication machinery and makes multiple copies of the virus. These burst out of cells and infection starts to spread. Antibodies generated by the immune system target this virus and, in most cases, halt its progress. COVID-19 infection is mild and remains hidden, and keeps spreading in persons and those who come in contact. SARS, in fact, is harsher and kills one in ten patients. These symptoms appear soon, and the patient is admitted to a hospital, gets treatment, and the chain is broken. The worst happens when the virus travels down to respiratory tracks to the lungs, richer in Ace2 receptors. Sometimes, the body's immune system drives it there to attack. In an overresponse to an attacking virus, at times it causes inflammation. This is known as a "cytokine storm" (where *cyto* means cell, and *kine* means movement). In some cases, it can kill a patient.

Can it recur? In a cured patient, it can appear seasonally like the flu. But for a short period, the body develops immunity by forming antibodies against it. A vaccine will be a total cure. About it, Dr Skimer says that vaccine development work is on, on a war-front basis. Volunteers and companies are all grinding it hard. We may expect a vaccine in 2020 itself.

Day 25

18 April 2020, Saturday

Italy sees a sharp drop in ICU patients after stricter lockdown measures across the country. Germany is broadly testing for antibodies as a citizen to assess the spread. They are perhaps the first ones to carry out such a measure. Iran has lifted the lockdown from Tehran, the capital city. A rare picture of a couple sitting across a table in a restaurant was seen. Lockdown downsides are emerging now; Spanish parents are protesting to let their kids out for play. The woman who organised a protest against the lockdown in New York was arrested. In Kruger National Park, lions were spotted sleeping and resting on roads, since ongoing lockdown has prevented any humans from going out of their homes for many days now. The world is also eager to open up and take measures post-lifting lockdown.

A virology lab in Wuhan has denied any role of laboratories in fabricating or unleashing coronavirus. In India, the situation is pretty much the same, with an average of one thousand new cases being added for the past almost a week now.

More than one thousand three hundred new cases added up in twenty-four hours in India. It's a new high for Indian cases. It's the twenty-fifth day of the official lockdown in India. But actually, for almost more than a month now, people have been indoors.

Perhaps India locked down in nick of time, and hence not so

overwhelming numbers still. The big question of today is "is herd immunity effective?": whether people got infected, and with mild or no symptoms they recovered, and already have antibodies in them now. This is what German scientists are after. They say the initial containment is necessary to avoid super spread. And that then it's not so deadly; as seen, only about 0.3–0.4% of those infected die. Almost everywhere, the major discussion among people is whether the world will be the same if we go past COVID-19, or whether it is going to go sooner. As of now, it appears that people might have to live with it, for a while at least.

Day 26

19 April 2020, Sunday

Whenever there is an endemic or pandemic disease in the world, immediately there is talk of doomsday or apocalypse. The corona, COVID-19 scare of 2020 is no different world over; there is once again a talk of Mayan calendar predictions about the end of the world. Prophecies from the Bible about ten pandemics that will end the world. The famous Nostradamus of France cannot be left behind. People cite his five hundred years early prophecy of a disease that would emerge in China and ravage a country with twin peaks (most say it's Italy). Well, mysteries have always been around mankind since its origin. Even the big bang theory, the theory of evolution, or the selection of the fittest. All have always been questioned by others. Religion and science have always existed together in brethren and in animosity. Each tries to learn from the other. Each trying to discredit the other. Menfolk have always been in prayers as well as in labs.

In the real-time world now in India, when the day has ended: seventeen thousand two hundred and ninety-six confirmed cases with a new daily high (one thousand five hundred and seventy-three new cases added). Thirteen thousand eight hundred and eighty-three are active cases, two thousand eight hundred and fifty-four have recovered and five hundred and fifty-nine are deceased. There were protests across US cities to end the lockdown. And the death toll in Europe has gone above one hundred thousand. Saudi Arabia's highest religious body, the council of senior scholars, has urged Muslims worldwide to stay at home for prayers during Ramadan. Trump has warned China of the consequences for being "knowingly responsible" for the coronavirus pandemic, as the US's confirmed cases topped seven hundred and thirty thousand and fatalities in the country approached thirty-nine thousand. India, Albania, South Korea, Brazil, the US, and Europe all are mulling over options for laxer lockdown, as millions of people are rendered jobless. The number of new cases continues to drop across Spain, France, and Italy. The UK seems the same. Iran is opening up a little lockdown. The jokes on corona have receded and a serious gloom has taken over social media. Now almost every household is worried about the future of kids' school and regular pay of family members. Many have lost jobs too. The airline has rested almost all of its staff. Except for social distancing and lockdown, no assurance has come out from the medical fraternity world over.

Day 27

20 April 2020, Monday

I founded an NGO, about four years ago, by the name of EK Haryana, named after my home state, "Haryana". We collected about sixty-one thousand Rupees from its members and purchased PPE worth the same: masks, sanitizers, gloves, aprons, shields. We will give the same to Deputy Collector Mr Amit Khatri tomorrow, the D.C of Gurugram. A meeting was arranged by my friend, Justice Sudhir Parmar. I shall go along with friends and members of this NGO tomorrow to facilitate distribution through government authorities to the policeman, medics, and other needy staff. Everyone in these desperate times is pitching in and fighting it out at his or her level. Famous Indian business tycoon Mr Ratan Tata has pledged a donation of one thousand five hundred Crore and let his famous Taj Hotel in Mumbai be used by doctors and other staff. The march of COVID-19 spread is on in India at a pace of now above one thousand two hundred cases per day.

Now a few things about the lockdown: its purpose, its efficiency, and it's nonsense. For the last some four months now, people are hearing, seeing, talking, and living these things. The lockdown, quarantines, social distancing, masks, gloves, sanitizers, etc.

Social distance was supposed to be more than one to five metres. But practically all broke it. Policemen, among colleagues and while checking others for medics, paramedics; it's a luxury if they come to maintain. But they cannot. Each person who goes to a shop, for example, a grocery, which is among the essential services kept open, will have to come within one metre to exchange the payment and pick up stuff. Security guards, among themselves and while checking others in society gates. How much will you sanitize a residential lift used twenty-four seven by more than one thousand people day and night? People do go out for walks, for fetching essentials. Then, there are their cluster of slums where labourers live; it is impossible to see social distancing there. They have a single toilet for more than one hundred men, women, kids, and the elderly. Then, deliveries to home via packets, doorknobs, staircases, car parking, shoes – what will you sanitize? In my opinion, it might have bought some time but that's it. Only people who are forced indoors, people living in high-rise societies, even they come out for walks, legal or illegal I don't know. The rest, independent houses, people in villages and in slums almost all have free access to roads, farms, etc.

Harvest season is around and now all will be open fields to harvest thrash and carry. Soon, all will have to go to the market to sell. The worst sufferers are daily labourers, contractual workers, part-timers, and small shopkeepers. And to some extent people in the private sector. The hospitals are refusing to take and treat patients other than COVID-19 infected ones, in many a place. Newspapers are not reaching most people. Basic stuff like milk is also a luxury now. People get roughed up by the police if seen on roads. Lockdown was clamped and many migratory labourers suffered worst; these were cases of some walking for ten to fifteen days on foot to their homes. Some were beaten up and quarantined by force by police. And there was a case of a labourer not getting to eat anything, and committing suicide. So much of a lockdown. It is killing people mentally already. Soon it will start killing in real life, when there will be no income left in households. I will update the number around the world for cases tomorrow.

Day 28

22 April 2020, Tuesday

Towards the close of the day of 21st April 2020. Nothing, yet again, changed for the day. I got special permission from the administration and, along with three more friends and a member of my NGO 'Ek Haryana', was allowed to go and hand over PPE kits, masks, sanitizer, etc. that we had the day earlier procured from member friends of our NGO. It was about three thousand masks, one hundred sanitizer bottles, and about two hundred complete PPE kits, all handed over to district 'D' commissioner Mr Amit Khatri, who thanked us and ensured a correct distribution by his staff. It was an opportunity to see the outside world also after a month. The roads had police pickets, and most turned into one-way. Every vehicle was stopped by policemen in masks, to ask about credentials. Only essential services are allowed. The secretariat had a few people, officials only. A tunnel was made at the entrance, which had showers fitted in the same, and every passer-by is disinfected in the shower with sanitizer before entering the premises. There was clear weariness and worried expressions on all faces. No one touches no one, over-scared to sit on seats.

Not too much to rejoice over again on the COVID-19 front. India had a new high of a rise of one thousand five hundred and thirty-seven cases in a single day. Now, total cases have gone past twenty thousand in India. The total number was twenty thousand and eighty confirmed, fifteen thousand four hundred and sixty active, three thousand nine hundred and seventy-five recovered, and six hundred and forty-five deceased. And in the world, all total cases are two million, five hundred and thirty-six thousand six hundred and seventy-three: one hundred and seventy-five thousand seven hundred and fifty-nine deaths, and six hundred and eighty-six thousand two hundred and twelve recovered. USA: eight hundred and four thousand seven hundred and fifty-nine total cases, four thousand nine hundred and ninety-five total deaths. Total cases rose by twelve thousand in the USA. World Food Programme reports that deaths due to hunger will double this year. Apart from a medical emergency, now economies are planning for economic emergencies too. The crude prices are at rock bottom, at their lowest ever: gone down to below zero $/per barrel. In fact, negative in Canada. If this pandemic goes on for a year or two, there is absolutely no doubt that the dark ages will begin on earth. India was supposed to open up a little after 20th April, but it has not happened so far and people now look up to 3rd May, the next date to lift the lockdown. But most are heartbroken and feel it will not be lifted even then, as cases keep mounting every day.

Day 29

22 April 2020, Wednesday

The continuity of the same routine over and over and over again leaves one low and dried of newness. My pen's ink freezes at times, writing the same thing over and over and over again. The views from the balcony simply refuse to change from a blank road, to hustle and bustle of women, kids, men, school buses, hawkers, suppliers, vendors, repair crew, electricians, and plumbers; all have simply vanished in thin air.

There is big chaos the world over, not only in India. Debates rage on symptoms, cure, vaccine development, and causes of this time-stopping virus COVID-19. There are pollution levels dropping in all places. Noise, smoke, all pollutants are gone. Some respite for wild animals, strays, and birds. But the cost that is paid is the freedom of the entirety of mankind. All are shunted out of normal life. The day in India ended with one thousand two hundred plus new cases. Cases in Italy, Spain, and France have drastically dropped, but are not over yet. New Zealand and Australia hardly have any new cases. So are China, South Korea, South Africa, and other African nations okay too?

But all these countries and the entire globe have come to a grinding halt. As if someone pressed an "emergency stop" switch, without warning. The UK, Aussies, Germany, Israel, China, USA – all seem to be heading towards an elusive vaccine. If on the fast track, we might have one by the middle of next year.

And at present, the future of schools, colleges, and many other institutes is uncertain. The normal life of going to a restaurant on a date and hugging and kissing your date might be a far-off thing. People have gotten accustomed to a greeting by "Namaste", by folding both hands against the chest, slightly bowing and uttering "Namaste", which means I bow to your soul and I respect you. Handshakes, will not come back so soon. Maybe masks and gloves are future tools to go to social gatherings till a vaccine is available. Once again, I am letting go of figures of death and cases, will update you tomorrow on it.

Day 30

23 April 2020, Thursday

India is continuously mounting new highs of cases infected with COVID-19. It was one thousand six hundred and sixty-seven newly added cases, taking the total tally of cases to twenty-three thousand and thirty-nine, seventeen thousand three hundred and six active cases, five thousand and twelve recovered (six hundred and forty-two recovered today), seven hundred and twenty-one deceased. Maharashtra is leading in the infamous Mumbai of city's cases of corona. Six thousand four hundred and twenty-seven total cases now in Maharashtra. There is talk of a new vaccine being developed in the UK. Elisa Granato was the first volunteer to get injected with the trial vaccine in the UK. This vaccine was developed in the last three months by a team at Oxford University.

Sarah Gilbert, professor of vaccinology at the Jenner Institute, led the pre-clinical research. Prof. Gilbert is highly hopeful of positive results from this vaccine. A small bit of information on "how the vaccines work". The vaccine is made from a weakened version of a common cold virus (known as adenovirus) from chimpanzees that have been modified. So, it cannot grow in humans. Basically, scientists have taken genes for the spike protein on the surface of coronavirus and put them into a harmless virus to make a vaccine. This is injected into the patient. The vaccine enters the cells, which then start to produce the coronavirus spike protein. This prompts the immune system to produce antibodies and activates killer T-cells to destroy infected cells. If the patient encounters the coronavirus again, the antibodies and T-cells are triggered to fight the virus.

The Oxford team had already developed a vaccine against 'MERS', a coronavirus, using similar techniques. Prof. Andrew Pollard, director of Oxford vaccine group, is heading the trial. In other news: Sinovac Biotech has created a new COVID–19 vaccine by growing the novel coronavirus in the Vero monkey cell live and inactivating it with chemicals. It is said to be protecting these Rhesus macaque monkeys from coronavirus. After the 16th of April, human trials begin. The situation all around remains the same. There is large scepticism and low confidence in the lifting of partial lockdown by all countries. Until a vaccine arrives to rescue, we all are hanging out there in hope.

Day 31

24 April 2020, Friday

Zombies have become us. When the day began, when it passed into noon, evening, and night. Time has come to a halt. And it's no exaggeration that 6 to 8 and maybe more hours people and kids spend on small and big screens, watching series, and movies at time classes. There is no let-up still on CORONA Spread. Again, there were fourteen-hundred plus cases added in India. But two Indian states Tripura and Goa have declared themselves CORONA-free. Kerala, and Haryana, are fast coming out of it. In fact, Manipur too has Zero cases now. Maharashtra, Delhi, Tamil Nadu, Rajasthan, Madhya Pradesh, and Andhra are front runners.

A new symptom has emerged called "COVID toes" in kids and some patients. Reported first in Italy, the USA too confirmed it. Doctors have seen "clots" formation and not bursting of cells as seen before in some cases – a cause of death in many. In India, still it is spreading and causing much havoc, though less when compared to Europe and USA. WHO feels it now also has become a human rights issue due to the long lockdown and people losing jobs and employers cutting salaries at these times. Even central government employers in India are set to lose their travel allowance and Dearness allowances. The salary hikes will also be affected. Many private companies have already laid off staff; soon now courts are bound to be flooded with companies for compensation and unemployment. Human rights issues shall emerge and will life remain safe same from now on? This is the major doubt in people's minds. No other single disease thus far baffled a common man's, a scientist's, or a doctor's mind so much as COVID–19. There are said to be many strains attacking now. Theories abound about the mutation capability of this virus. It might assimilate psychological abilities to cope with many. There is no talk, no news, nothing in lives either of this disease or its associated impacts on lives.

Day 32

25 April 2020, Saturday

The holy month of Ramzan, also called Ramadan, has begun. And the world over, Islamic spiritual leaders stay and pray indoors. It's now more than a month or two since all mosques, temples, Gurudwaras, and other places of religious gatherings are totally shut. All pilgrimages are halted all over. This simply highlights for the believer of God that; he is inside or not outside. The situation continues to worsen for India again; one thousand eight hundred and thirty-five new cases were added, making a total of twenty-six thousand two hundred and eighty-three confirmed cases, nineteen thousand five hundred and nineteen active, five thousand nine hundred and thirty-nine recovered and eight hundred and twenty-five deceased. Maharashtra alone has eight hundred and eleven new case today.

In my city, Gurugram, there were paramedics and medics from a hospital named Medanta. Doctors, nurses, and medics are sacrificing so much for all, it's worth praising. The news was doing rounds that P.G.I. medical Chandigarh has successfully treated six patients with some medicine/vaccine, which is new and not known so far. More confirmations might come tomorrow on the same. Spain now has more recoveries of their new cases, so it's good news.

In Italy, per day, death has dropped, but new cases are still adding up to have a total of around three thousand. World over:

two million, nine hundred and eight thousand two hundred and six cases, two hundred and two thousand five hundred and one deaths, and eight hundred and thirty-two thousand two hundred and eleven recovered. The USA has had fifty-three thousand seven hundred and forty-five deaths. Spain: twenty-two thousand nine hundred and two deaths. Italy: twenty-six thousand three hundred and eighty-four deaths. France: twenty-two thousand six hundred and fourteen deaths. The UK: twenty thousand three hundred and nineteen deaths. The list goes on. There is a serious worry now gripping India about the economy and lockdown – how to strike a balance? The prime minister will again hold a meeting with all chief ministers on the 27th of April. But Chief Minister Yogi Adityanath of Uttar Pradesh, the most populous state of India, has extended the lockdown up to 3rd June. We can clearly now see that we are only a poor and half a developing country, when help measures are compared to the USA or Australia etc. who are providing monetary help to their citizens, employed or unemployed, just to stay home and make their ends meet. In Australia, the tenants are free of rent for the next six months. The country is caught in a bind; all the industries, and factories, construction activities are in big cities like Delhi, Mumbai, Noida, Gurugram, Chennai, etc. and all the big cities are in red zones.

India is divided into green, orange, and red zones as per the severity of COVID–19 infections. The activities that can take place for industries are those out of the red zone. There might be some changes, same in this approach, in the coming week. Now it is a wait-and-watch situation. Will people tire out sitting at home or they can stay indoors for another month or two?

Day 33

26 April 2020, Sunday

Economy versus lockdown. The world over. After the nation has endorsed lockdown from weeks to months. It's clearly affecting jobs, businesses, the lives. The USA, Spain, Italy, France, Korea, and China are almost on the brink to reopen partially. Developing nations will stop now; it's inevitable. There cannot be an endless state of lockdown, and people cannot keep on losing jobs or lives in a state of peril. Even when the vaccine is not available, countries will have to open. Spain, for the first time, had death below three hundred, and this rejoices there. After the demand of parents in Spain, kids below fourteen, too, shall be allowed to go play outside for one hour daily. And in India, the increase in number, but definitely cases in still on rising. We have not seen the top still. One thousand six hundred patients were added today but five hundred and eighty-five got cured too. It appears to slow down in Maharashtra; for the first time in the last few days, there was a figure below five hundred for new cases. The job is on at a frantic pace for developing a vaccine for COVID-19 coronavirus: eighty-three companies are in a race, with six companies going onto the human trial stage and seventy-seven at the pre-clinical stage.

This is the fastest response to develop a vaccine, say experts. Before this, the mumps vaccine was developed in 1967 in four years' time. In India: Zydus, Cadila, Serum Institute of India,

Biological E, Bharat Biotech, Indian Immunological ltd. On a very positive note, the vaccine could be there by October 2020, and life back to normal by 2021.

Day 34

27 April 2020, Monday

I write as per mood swings and as per news unfolds. The news is now only one a day. I am wondering how lovers are coping in lockdown. They cannot call, especially if they are part-time lovers or illicit lovers, as the legal spouse surrounds their counterparts. Tough on debauchery. The way online games, activities, and e-commerce are promoted, will already add to inactive, computer-savvy generations' laziness. The pets are another bunch of sufferers, as their walks in the evening and mornings are cut off or drastically reduced. I remember seeing people in masks in 2015; SARS was active then.

I never feared that it would hit me. And honestly, I sort of pitied or mocked the people wearing masks. But now the same me is shit scared stepping out without a mask on. Touching is a forbidden fruit now. I hope masks do not stay forever, and hugs make a comeback too, post-corona.

Dr Jett Kwong from Toronto University says, "In case of lack of a vaccine for COVID-19, a certain portion of the population needs to become infected to develop what's known as herd immunity, in order to end the pandemic." So what is "Herd immunity"? So, in herd immunity, suppose there are many who had this disease and are immune to it now due to sufficient antibodies present in them. It will break the chain of spread and eventually stop it totally.

India witnessed the largest number of single-day fatalities with sixty, and one thousand four hundred and sixty-three more new cases added. The world's total number of infected confirmed cases has gone above three million now. New Zealand's prime minister, Jacinda Ardern, announces that it has stopped community transmission, and effectively eliminated the virus. The count of the new case has come to a single digit. Plasma therapy is now also done in India, and the capital Delhi has seen good results. Six patients from Markaj, Delhi Tabhlighi Zamaat have recovered from corona in a hospital in Lucknow. And they have vowed to help doctors, as much as they can. They have gone on to donate their blood or take vaccine trial shots; whatever is required to help stop this spread. Science seems to have won some hearts. It feels good to read such positive news. After all, we are all same humans who can lead, mislead, and can be led. May hope remains in all hearts.

Day 35

28 April, Tuesday

Seclusion, isolation, deprivation of freedom, cornered, quarantined, lockdown or up, whatever you may name it. It has a pattern that affects all, a similar type of pattern. As I said earlier, I am a sailor, a seaman, and a marine engineer. I have been at sea since 1996. The longest stretch that I have been on a ship was ten months. In the same cabin, the same ship, where at times I didn't go ashore for more than two months, meaning that I had stayed confined on the ship itself. Well, there have been instances of men at sea staying two to three years continuously sailing on the same ship. In fact, I had sailed and met a few in my sailing career. I am narrating time, so as to share and compare my experiences of being locked down in ships and locked down first time in my forty-five years at home. When you join a ship, you leave your family and go and control to serve your ship, your company. First week, you are lost; you have lots of days for yourself. You wake up in your ship's cabin, and you thought that you were at home. It baffles the mind. A feeling of helplessness creeps in, a feeling that you cannot escape. Then slowly, you get familiarized with your cabin, with your ship, and immerse yourself in an hourly routine to pass time. You literally break up a day in small bits to pass time. If you try to swallow a whole day quickly, it doesn't happen. So, you have these small routines, like a compulsory morning tea on Bridge. Then breakfast by seven a.m., then the morning day's scheduled work order. And then tea at ten a.m., then round up half day at twelve p.m., lunch at twelve p.m. to one p.m., a small walk past lunch for fifteen minutes, write half day summary and report to the office and afternoon siesta. Three p.m. tea, up to three-thirty p.m. A walk for an hour then till 1630. Round-up the day's work by five p.m. Six p.m.: exercise and shower. Seven p.m.: dinner time. Seven p.m. to eight p.m.: the rounds, reports making, reporting. Eight p.m. to ten p.m. on Bridge: tea, gossip, walk for thirty minutes. By ten p.m., retire to cabin and watch a movie till twelve a.m., then sleep. And repeat for four to six months and your duty is done.

I applied the same during my lockdown at home for almost thirty-seven, and thirty-eight days now. I break up my day in portions and pass time. For example, now I start the day at ten a.m. with tea till ten-thirty a.m. News and morning updates of messages on social media for an hour. Eleven-thirty a.m. to twelve p.m.: brunch. Then two hours straight of the Netflix series. It goes up to about two-thirty p.m. Then shower by three-thirty p.m. and bed for siesta up to five p.m. Five p.m. to five-thirty p.m.: write a daily diary. Five-thirty p.m. to six-thirty p.m.: exercise. Six-thirty p.m.: evening tea till seven p.m. Seven p.m. to nine p.m.: hit TV again. Dinner and walk of an hour and conclude by eleven p.m., social media till twelve a.m., write again for thirty to forty minutes, read before sleep and sleep by two a.m. and repeat. So that's lockdown here; quite similar to ship. It's all in the head. All in thoughts, you can enjoy your day, any day for that matter, anywhere. The longer you stay at home, the fonder you are of little things around your home which you never noticed earlier. It's time to introspect, heal, evolve, and be future-ready. COVID–19 is still there. I track it twice daily, less news. I won't delve into negative news. But yes, it is there all around. Today one thousand nine hundred and three cases added in India. Cases slowed down in Europe but not going, I would say. Miraculously, New Zealand, Australia, and South Korea ducked it without much pain and their currencies are flourishing even in troubled times. Developed countries have reserves. It's poor Asia and Africa who will once again take a beating.

Day 36

The thought that haunts me most nowadays is: will this year and next year or maybe till we have a working vaccine against COVID-19 be wiped out of our lives? With no real-time outings, no schools for kids, no handshakes, no hugs, no movies, no outings, no celebration for marriages, or no mourning for the dead. Even the thought of going in closer proximity to another fellow human is sinful. God knows how soon things will improve, or will they actually improve? When I tell friends that all will be okay soon, most reply, "No it won't be the same ever again". The rate of spread is the same in India for almost a week: one thousand five hundred to one thousand nine hundred new cases are added, almost four hundred get cured daily and the death total now is over one thousand.

Daily routines are topsy-turvy now. A mighty county like the US is at the centre of pity for other nations. Total cases are a whopping one million, fifty-five thousand three hundred and three in the states, and deaths now number sixty-one thousand one hundred and twelve. One hundred and forty-four thousand four hundred and twenty-three have recovered too. In India, cases are now up to thirty-one thousand seven hundred and eighty-seven and one thousand and eight deaths. Hospitalized patients who recovered using Remdesivir recovered faster, as per a US agency.

Another area of life that will be hit hard is sports. The Olympics was due in 2020, but will not be until July 2025. God only knows if it will be held. Football, cricket and all other sports are just cancelled now. Even a sportsperson cannot train. This miserable disease has crippled each and every sphere of life. Many promising sportspersons who would have just peaked for the 2020 Olympics and other sports they were training hard for 2020 will be hit.

Gyms and swimming pools might open very late. On the good news front, Mr Poonawala, CEO of "Serum" (an Indian company that makes vaccines) has said they would be ready with the first batch of Oxford vaccine (UK based) and would charge one thousand Rs (about ten pounds). They are also improving BCG vaccines, as a recombinant, to aid ineffectiveness against COVID–19. A German company, too, has begun human trials of their vaccine against COVID-19. The vaccine serum that the company is producing has been successful on animals. The race has not up as to who will produce the vaccine first.

Day 37

30 April 2020, Thursday

My mind wanders off to when there were no viruses or pandemics. When man was a hunter, a food gatherer, a caveman, or, in recent history, when modern allopathic science had not developed. So how did they contain, or is that they used to simply perish in hordes and survival of the fittest? Who would have guided them? Nature? And what about today? Are we winning the fight against COVID-19? Or it will simply vanish on its own? Do we just slow it down? Can we duck a viral invasion, which is all around in the air, in micro invisible tiny air suspension that can be blown away by air and transmitted? Do we all get infected and only those who have better immunities make it alive? How effective are vaccines? Are they a one hundred per cent sure shot method of prevention?

This stale, locked-up lifestyle, if it becomes perpetual in our lives, doesn't sound very healthy. I want to stay away once again from the numbers of dying humans, of infected poor humans. It appalls me a lot, daily shutting down, searching for some good news. First of all, there is no name at all except coronavirus, COVID–19.

But in India, we are yet to know which way we are heading. When will we peak in cases and a decline thence forth? Now Sinovac, a Chinese company, says that they are ready with 'CoronaVac' after success with treating monkeys. They have begun testing on humans too, and say man production will be ready soon to the tune of one hundred thousand per year. In Russia, PM Mishustin tests positive for the virus. After opening lockdown in Wuhan, China, they are still struggling to come back to normal life. Shopkeepers say they have zero profits. Fearful people avoid each other. Now some say it will be three years to normalize totally. Inactive days are killing dreams. Hope for a new day tomorrow. Good night.

Day 38

1 May 2020, Friday

It was International Labour Day, the 1ˢᵗ of May. Ironically, most labourers around the world had no labour and no work to do. There are sporadic instances of suicides, and mass suicides due to hunger due to unemployment. We in India had never prepared for social security. In fact, the concept only doesn't exist. So, in times of COVID-19 crisis, we are hapless, helpless, sitting ducks, except for a mockery of a lockdown. We have no measures for providing food to all, barring a few occasions and not to all. And forget about unemployment payments, bonuses, or provisions like those in developed countries. As expected, the lockdown in India is extended by two more weeks; the date of 3ʳᵈ May which was the last day of lockdown is now changed to 17ᵗʰ May 2020.

The fear just gets deeper. It stays and doesn't go away at all. The little bit of loosening to lockdown in the last days is just for the namesake. Only essential services are on. Food, healthcare, banking, etc. A few IT companies and other companies asked about thirty per cent of staff to come to offices in personal vehicles. Public transport is off. Construction and some factories are allowed to work with restrictions, but barely any labor is available now. Fear is so deep; all migratory labour has fled. The remaining will be at the first opportunity of opening up restrictions. The scenario in India is different from that of Europe or America. People here are more scared, due to perhaps less trust in healthcare facilities. Each coming day robbed Indians of anything that was nice. Like all shopping malls, gyms, sports activities, cinemas, and even social gatherings like marriages and other activities slowly, slowly all tapered down and now it's nil. Until there is a vaccine, the trust of people will not be restored. The Government has no plans at all to bring back labourers; how will they assure of the security of food, and jobs? It will again be a private player who will resume at their own risk, if at all.

WHO confirms now that the coronavirus COVID–19 is not a man or laboratory-synthesized; it has developed biologically, naturally. Despite US research confirming WHO's stand, the president, Mr Trump, still believes it is a Chinese lab's brainchild. Today, there was a new peak in India, and for the first time, new infected positive cases surpassed two thousand. In Maharashtra alone, one thousand and eight cases were reported. People are restless already. There is resentment building toward forced lockdown. One of my friends ended up saying India has enough people, so what if a million are lost? It will not make any difference. Herd immunity will be the only solution, he feels. Europe is now slowly opening up cautiously in phases. India might open up only in June/July, as it stands. Let's see. My kids have not met their friends now for almost forty days. I don't think it's fair at all. Nature has totally gripped humanity in fear.

Day 39

2 May 2020, Saturday

Bad times see resentment in people and hope; also, I believe the phoenix rises from the ashes only. I talk about myself since the first news of the coronavirus and to date. I immediately knew, when news from Wuhan started to trickle in India, and the first batch of overseas patients (actually tourists) from Jaipur, all Italian, and their Indian driver tested positive, that days of tremendous change have knocked upon me, upon us.

I visualise a world post-corona: the restaurants will have more drive-ins, served in personal cars or small sanitized cubicles for families. Entries and exits are marked for social distancing. There might be neon displays in restaurants, showing whose number it is to enter. People will keep waiting in cars till then. Robots might serve. Bookings for seats will be online. Home delivery might pick up. Delivery boys might carry a corona negative certificate, recently acquired. They might come with thermal guns to show that they have no fever prior to delivery. Households might make permanent sanitizer entrances with sprinkler showers.

Namaste might be an international way of greeting, like hello. Funerals will be more mechanized use of incinerators for burning the dead. Strangers will not be welcome to make contacts, never physically at least. There might come a methodology to prove the food served is virus and bacterial-free.

Restaurants might need newer tools to keep their certificate licenses to serve valid, like sanitizing tunnels at entrances. Social distancing met with a spacing of tables, and seats. Cabs will have to keep sanitizer. There might be curtains blocking the driver and passengers. All will be carrying their fitness certificate handy. Seasonal drugs will be available to boost immunity against viruses. Passengers might need inoculation against corona for travel, like yellow fever, etc.

My head was in a muddle. I overthink perhaps, but cannot help it. Now the race for a vaccine against COVID-19. Eight probable vaccines have gone on to human trials, Moderna, Johnson & Johnson, Oxford research, Serum Biotechnologies, etc. are a few, apart from China's Sinovac and German research compacts. Vaccine looks sure shot available by the end of 2021, at the earliest maybe the end of 2020. The rate of spread has increased in India and is catching up fast with the more severely affected nations, though the mortality rate remains low in India. Total cases confirmed: thirty-nine thousand six hundred and ninety-nine. Total added today: two thousand four hundred and thirty-seven. Active cases: twenty-seven thousand five hundred and fifty-three. Recovered: ten thousand eight hundred and nineteen. Deceased: one thousand three hundred and twenty-three. In the world today, total number of cases is three million, four hundred and seventy thousand two hundred and seventy-seven. Deaths are up to two hundred and forty-three thousand nine hundred and sixty-six, and one million, one hundred and fourteen thousand one hundred and sixty-four have recovered. The USA has one million, one hundred and fifty-four thousand nine hundred and thirty-one cases. Today, twenty-three thousand nine hundred and one new cases were added. Total deaths number sixty-seven thousand and ninety-nine, with one thousand three hundred and forty-six deaths today. In Spain: two hundred and forty-five thousand five hundred and sixty-seven cases, with two thousand five hundred and eighty-eight added today. Twenty-five thousand one hundred deaths, two hundred and seventy-six new deaths. Italy: two hundred and nine thousand three hundred and twenty-eight cases, twenty-eight thousand seven hundred and ten deaths, with four hundred and seventy-nine deaths today and one thousand nine hundred new cases. UK: one hundred and eighty-two thousand two hundred and sixty cases, with four thousand eight hundred and six additions today. Two thousand eight hundred and thirty-one deaths, with six hundred and twenty-one deaths today. Tomorrow will be the fortieth day when I am writing daily updates of my life and others. I hope only to pass on updates, so that some may benefit, and some may know of these days we actually lived.

Day 40

Coronavirus, the COVID–19 variant of coronavirus, is proving to be an enigma. A puzzle for scientists and doctors all over the world. The best minds in medicine are intrigued by this virus's effects. The latest in the series is the "happy hypoxia" effect seen on patients. Normal saturation with oxygen of the lung is ninety-five per cent. Low cases at eighty and seventy per cent saturation will cause uneasiness and discomfort. Patients with fifty per cent saturation have walked in and behaving normally. A case of thirty per cent saturation was reported in a UK-based hospital, where a female patient said "she is feeling cold". Doctors are finding it bizarre and unseen previously. Now, Russia saw its biggest single-day rise of ten thousand cases. In India, every coming day, numbers are increasing and today, again, is a new high. India now has forty-two thousand five hundred and five cases, one thousand three hundred and ninety-one deaths, and eleven thousand seven hundred and seventy-five people who have recovered. In Madagascar, a new drug is being sold, said to cure COVID–19. It's a drug made from a plant called Artemisia, plant used in making anti-malaria drugs. A herbal cure. Though it's tested on less than twenty patients, it's named 'COVID organics.

Michael Pompeo, from US secretary of state, says they have enormous evidence against China's lab-made virus. Doctors in

Italy warn that antibody testing is no panacea or ticket to freedom from corona. Doctors say they don't know how long they last. Different antibody levels have been found in different patients who recovered, and they are yet to establish a benchmark as to how much is a safer level of antibodies.

A global blowback is building against China now. Many countries seek inquiry into the origin of the virus. Some are planning to seek to file compensation from China. UK and Germany are wary of working with tech giant Hua Wei. The Irish band U2 have given ten million for the research and development of drugs to fight corona. Remdesivir & hydroxychloroquine are two medicines which can be effective that I read mentions of daily. People are gearing up at the moment to learn to live with the coronavirus score. Most of the affected countries are planning to open up in phases. India has not peaked yet it seems; time only will tell. The liquor vendors will be open. Booze lovers cherish this news.

Day 41

4 May 2020, Monday

The COVID-19 remains a mystery to be solved. Now there is news making the rounds, of wrong prognosis and diagnosis. That the virus causes clot formation and thrombosis, which is the main cause of death. Meanwhile, India's first day of easing up the lockdown saw kilometers-long queues to fetch liquor. Social distancing has gone for a toss. People have emerged from their homes and are in markets and on roads. A wee bit of socializing has resumed too. Results of these might be catastrophic, or plain with no inferences to spread infections. India saw a tremendous leap in cases, a new high again of three thousand five hundred and above, with Maharashtra alone going up one thousand five hundred cases in a day. In France, Spain, and Italy, cases are dropping now. Russia remains rising. Indonesia is ravaged, but neighbour Malaysia is much less affected. It will be seen later why the virus spreads so much in one country and not so in others. Is it social distancing, is it hygiene, is its temperature? Or eating habits? All remains to be seen yet.

Day 42

5 May 2020, Tuesday

The spread is the same in India: two thousand nine hundred plus cases today. New cases in Europe are dropping. Israel says that they have already developed an antidote for COVID-19. Amidst a severely infected world, India takes a brave call to repatriate stranded Indians back home. I term it a foolish decision. They could have waited a month or two. But I am no government here. The similar chilling decision is taken in India by sending back millions of labourers and workers to their home state, via trains. The disaster of a recipe, or recipe for disaster, whatever you may call it. Another foolish decision was to open liquor vendors all across India. Social distancing was blown away in an hour; there were kilometers-long queues and people piling upon each other to fetch a bottle. I fail to understand then why lock down at all for forty days, when, at peak of spread, they are opening up. Up to industries opening was okay, so that caution could be exercised and so the economy could be resumed. Italy, too, claims to have developed a vaccine, which they have tested in mice and produces sufficient antibodies to destroy COVID–19 infected cells. They are testing it on humans too shortly. So far, HIV and dengue-causing viruses have not had any vaccines developed against them. But this might be a new chapter in medicine if an effective vaccine arrives against COVID-19. The Oxford vaccine group and Oxford's Jenner Institute have an upcoming vaccine "chAdox1 n cov-19", which is based on the adenovirus vaccine vector and the SARS-CoV-2 spike protein. And they are leading among eight human-tested vaccines in a tray out of one hundred and two total players in the game trying to get a vaccine. The world has surpassed three point five million cases already. Three-quarters of these are in Europe and USA.

Day 43

6 May 2020, Wednesday

India continues to be on edge the last few days. It's a new high every day today again: three thousand five hundred plus new cases. News on the vaccine front is, in addition to the last two days of new developments from Israel, Italian scientists are also claiming a vaccine. It has already been tested in mice, and produces a good number of antibodies against COVID-19 – in fact, against various variants of the virus. Many countries are saying the virus may have mutated multiple times and maybe as many as thirty variants could be active. TV is only used to watch fun-filled exciting Netflix series. Except for COVID-19, there is no news on TV now. But people have started to come out for walks with precaution. Many are flaunting it too. It's a big commotion now the city is partially opening and cases are rising. In Haryana, my state, Gurgaon, where I reside, has a maximum number of cases. A vegetable market is a new hotbed now in Gurgaon, Bahadurgarh, a nearby town, and Azadpur, in Delhi. The Tabhlighi Zamat attendees were cursed by all about a month ago for not coming about social distancing. The same is now annihilated at the liquor store. God knows which way we are headed. Towards herd immunity or towards a wider spread. Life remains locked, partially somewhere, totally elsewhere.

Day 44

7 May 2020, Thursday

The worst part of being locked down is hopelessness, and uncertainty of tomorrow. Day after day has gone, yet nothing is known. And as news trickles of the death of a policeman, a young Amit Jatrana, of the Delhi police, his account of death by corona has shaken many. He hailed from Hulledi village of Sonipat. A young vivacious man, who left behind a wife, and a young son. He complained of breathlessness to his fellow policemen in the night. They gave him tea and warm water and took him early in hours morning to a hospital in Delhi, where there he was denied admission. And Amit died without getting any medical help. Only post-death was it ascertained that he was corona positive. And finally, the remains which were once Amit were incinerated unceremoniously in an electric crematorium without any last rites. He now is very well a sign of things around; the callous attitude of the Government. A young promising life cut short; both sad and scary. There is absolutely no flattening of the curve yet in India. And my days and nights are the same as billions of Indians. Nothing to do, nothing to hope for, nothing to look forward to. Just exist. At least we are lucky to get food on the table. My heart goes out to the ones who cannot even have that.

Day 45

8 May 2020, Friday

A Gurgaon-based Company, Premas Biotech, too has entered the race to produce vaccines for COVID-19. They say that "the multi-anti-genetic approach is being designed to try to overcome presently known and possible future mutations of novel coronavirus, which, if successful, would result in the development of an effective vaccine. Unlike single protein vaccines, they are developing a multi-sub-unit vaccine with three antigens. The vaccine contains Spike (s), Envelopes (E), and Membrane (M) Proteins in multiple formats" Dr Prabuddha Kundu, the MD of the company, gave this insight. They are going to head for animal trials soon. Without an antidote, without a vaccine, and no guarantee of a lack of recurrence of already cured patients. It paints an ambiguous picture. Some Ayurvedic immunity boosters are also suggested to everyone so as to keep one ready to combat corona, in case one gets it. I hope this bad dream fades away soon. Life without purpose is no life. What shall mankind dream of, if there is no freedom of living freely?

Day 46

9 May 2020, Saturday

India today stands at sixty-two thousand eight hundred and eight total confirmed cases: forty-one thousand four hundred and two active and nineteen thousand three hundred and one recovered. Also, two thousand one hundred and one are deceased. In the last twenty-four hours, two thousand eight hundred and ninety-four cases were added. Data from Delhi has not been added, as it has not updated. One thousand four hundred and fourteen have recovered, too. Also, one hundred and fifteen patients died. The world over, a total of four million, seventy-seven thousand nine hundred and fifty-five cases were confirmed, and two hundred and seventy-nine thousand and seventy-one deaths. One million, four hundred and twenty-five thousand and ninety were recovered. USA: one million, three hundred and thirty-nine thousand two hundred and ninety-eight total cases, with seventeen thousand five hundred and thirteen added in the last twenty-four hours. Seventy-nine thousand six hundred and twenty-seven total deaths, one thousand and twelve deaths in the last twenty-four hours. Spain, Italy, France, and Germany are recovering, the UK is still the same, and Russia has ten thousand new cases daily.

India is fast catching up with the front runners, with three thousand five hundred plus in cases daily. And life is at standstill. There is the hope of a vaccine with so many countries and companies labouring hard to be the first one. But the likelihood of vaccine is at the earliest at the end of the year and at the latest by the end of next year. But till then, it's an uncertain scenario. Fourteen days is a set parameter now to quarantine cases and suspected cases. After three negative reports, a patient is released. The unpredictable nature of this virus makes it hard to fight off. Diving in a swimming pool in summer is likely only in 2022 now.

Day 47

10 May 2020, Sunday

Today was, again, a day with the highest rise so far of new cases in a single day. It crossed four thousand plus cases. The lockdown by now has started to turn many folks into zombies. No one talks to anyone. No smiles are exchanged when you occasionally spot a stranger in markets (only the essential shops are open: medicine, milk, and vegetables). Touch is long gone. An accidental touch could wreak havoc on the mind. You would rush back home and wash thoroughly and change clothes too. By now, each household has masks, sanitizers, and sprays of disinfectants. Indian poverty, remained hidden in buildings under construction or in factories, now was seen by all on roads. Trains now are open for labourers to go to their native lands. There are scenes of barefoot walkers. People on cycles, on trucks, are seen. Labourers migrating in thousands from metropolitan cities. Sadly, sixteen labourers sleeping on a rail track at night got run over. The scenes were saddening: the chapattis made last night by them, along with rag-like, torn clothes, a torn one hundred R bill. These will haunt my mind long. The march of devastation continues.

Day 48

1 May 2020, Monday

Prime Minister Modi again had a virtual online meeting of all chief ministers. The roadmap after the 17th of May is being discussed. Most states will remain locked in May. But industries and construction activities might further be increased. Evacuation from abroad via flights has resumed.

Trains will be opened to fifteen cities from Delhi. The world has changed so fast. Now there is no talk of making money. Talk is about making ends meet. Talk is of survival. Talk is of freedom. Talk is of desire to roam freely again. Many would want to erase this year, 2020, from their memories. Schools and colleges will be last to open. There doesn't seem to be a vaccine before the end of the year. Ironically, the pollution level is low. The weather remains good. But there is no desire to cherish it. It seems that without freedom, can humanity survive? We must think of the freedom and rights of animals, and plants too similarly, if we are surviving in symbiosis with nature. I shall update the numbers tomorrow about the latest status of corona in various parts of the world.

Day 49

12 May 2020, Tuesday

How do various people cope with these crisis-filled days? Many of them turned back to their hometowns, thinking it will be safe. Some went back to their villages. In fact, rightly so, the metropolis cities like Delhi, Chennai, Mumbai, and Gurgaon bore the brunt of COVID-19; a maximum number of deaths and cases had been there only. The funny thing is people in villages guard entries to villages, but inside no social distancing is followed. In rural Haryana, the card-playing gangs and hookah-smoking gangs are much at ease with each other. Village barbers are still open, village shops are open. Typical of India, the middle class ends up suffering the most. All their neighbourhood shops, except ones controlled by police, are okay. No one can venture out, no socializing at all. Many often get beaten up by the police if seen on roads. No law is enforced in rural India, except the vigilantism of villagers. This lockdown is a strange experiment, only selectively made to be followed. Migrant laborers won't catch it, so let them be on roads, on buses, or on trains too.

Similarly, the expat population won't catch it; they just made them hop in planes and be brought back. After discovering that the first corona cases have come via flights only, this is strange. Big economic reforms are announced now by PM Modi, especially with stress on the self-reliant new India. It appears a timely and wisely-thought decision. In times of partially or wholly sealed international borders, one has to be self-reliant.

And numbers in India simply do not cease anywhere. Till now, we have seen no flattening of the curve.

Day 50

Bundesliga matches are returning and there will be live sports action, perhaps the first in the last three months. WHO warns against that. This endemic may stay with us. And we will have to learn to live with it. Yesterday, Modi announced a twenty million package stimulus to bail out the economy and bring industries back into action. My question is, will there be enough workers willing to risk lives to come out and work? My city, Gurugram, stays in the lead of coronavirus patients in Haryana. No breather. But still, much less compared to Pune, Mumbai, Delhi, etc. The second wave of COVID-19 patients has started now in Wuhan. After a month of no patients, six new patients tested positive again. A similar story from South Korea too. Will this virus ever go away? Now one must hope for a vaccine and for an antidote. Lives continue to choke indoors. Whosoever says it's fun should be locked up, even after the lockdown is lifted. With safety measures, the world will open up. And once we have the cure, we will be back to normal. I tell this to myself before hitting the bed at two a.m. of the next day.

Day 51

14 May 2020, Thursday

I thought of going out today, as I have been getting calls from a group of friends. The roads are clear now and the movement of vehicles eased up. One of my friends has been calling at a rendezvous for some days. So, I dared and ventured out. And on the way, I called another friend of mine to say hello from afar. So, I set out after good forty days from home for a real one-to-one meeting with friends. Rajesh Dahiya, my friend, showed upon his society gate along with his two dogs, male Sabo and a female pet. He came to walk them. I parked the car in front of the society on Sohna Road and at Vatika Chowk in Gurgaon. He came wearing a mask and so was I. I called him and we decided sitting in the car will be risking social distancing. So, we met outside and of course no handshake. He offered a smoke, carefully handed me over a fag, and no touching. The dogs were tugging on leashes. We sat on a bench safely afar and chatted and laughed. How strange life has become. Now we all are scared to meet each other. We both had sanitizers in our pockets, and masks and yet were scared even to chat. I said bye to him and wished him well. Now I went on to meet Mahesh Thareja, Sandeep Lamba, Amit & Devender, and Dr Ramesh Chand. They are my regular mates over hookah on normal days. Even today, we would sanitize the pipe and have it. These simple meetings with masks loosely hanging or dropping off creates greater scare than any pleasure to the senses. And I was back home. At night, I had a horrific dream about corona. I got scared of COVID-19 infection, and recalled all forty to fifty days of meeting with people. Sweaty, I woke up, checked my throat in the mirror, asked my wife to fetch me a glassful of warm water. I think life is disturbed for all in these ways. I didn't track news today, except once and it's the same.

Day 52

The routine stays the same, no matter what. All that scare of social distance is now less as I see out of my balcony. I see more couples out for walks, and people with their pets, and repairmen doing rounds in society. How can perfect social distancing be achieved for six months? A thought came to my mind. I feel, not possible. Already, there are protests against lockdowns in Europe and in America. WHO says learn to live with it. Private labs say we will get you the vaccine. Many more things, they surely will get one at earliest, as most economies are floundering now.

The medical economy will get fruitful benefits, especially from a vaccine against COVID-19 and a trusted antidote too. A race is on to reap the benefits from being first to provide. Morals are shaken in public, especially among the labour class. They fear the end is near for everything and have fled en masse. Pictures of men and women, bare feet, on cycles, on bullock carts, hitchhikers are common now, walkers and on trains. All the lockdown planning and social distancing have gone for a toss. Let's see how far and wide it spreads, since millions in the peaking time of disease are on roads. Will it help develop herd immunity? Let's see. Scenes are the same in neighbouring Pakistan, and Bangladesh too. This thing about coronavirus, the COVID-19, is so mind-boggling. Nothing is clear yet after almost five to six months since its origin. Where did it actually originate? Is herd immunity a real thing? Is there any antidote yet? Will there be a vaccine ever? Even symptoms, diagnoses, and findings all have a different version. The line of treatment too is different in different countries. Nothing should be established as standard yet. Cases have dwindled in Europe and some regions of the States. In India, not so, and still the same on average of about three thousand five hundred new cases added daily. There is certainly a new case in South Korea and China now; both were free from new cases for more than thirty days. Now, at least, Wuhan and some cities in South Korea have declared to be corona-free.

Day 53

16 May 2020, Saturday

Night now. When I sit to write, it's midnight. The day saw the single most rise in new cases today of four thousand five hundred plus; that's a new high now.

Confirmed cases now in India have shot up to ninety thousand six hundred and forty-eight, with four thousand seven hundred and ninety-two new cases added today. Fifty-three thousand five hundred and forty-eight active cases, three thousand nine hundred and seventy-nine recovered, one hundred and eighteen deceased today – total two thousand eight hundred and seventy-one now deceased. The world's total cases are four million, seven hundred and six thousand eight hundred and ninety. Deaths: thirty-four thousand nine hundred and eleven. Recovered: eight hundred and two thousand eight hundred and ninety-six. USA is still at the top with one million, five hundred and three thousand five hundred and sixty-nine cases, with one million, seventy-six thousand six hundred and thirty-two active now and nineteen thousand two hundred and eighty-four new cases. Total deaths: eighty-nine thousand four hundred and forty-two, with nine hundred and thirty-five new deaths added. Three hundred and thirty-seven thousand four hundred and ninety-five are totally recovered. Italy & France in Europe is a little better now, with less than one thousand new cases daily and fewer deaths than in India.

143

Ahmedabad and Mumbai are the worst hit. One thing is sure: the world has changed forever. The world before corona was different and the world when it opens post-corona will be different. These are the toughest months for us who are witnessing this global pandemic. An age of uncertainty. Less pollution and less freedom.

Day 54

17 May 2020, Sunday

It was the last day of lockdown number three, which, as expected, increased to 31st May now; the fourth time lockdown has been extended. The situation is worsening, at its peak now in India. Peak as of now, that is. The number touched almost five thousand today, again, the single highest increase in twenty-four hours. One thing that this period clearly highlighted is that we are not a developed nation, and there is a huge chunk of the population living below the poverty line. India witnessed the biggest trans-state migrations by roads, trains, private trunks, by cycles. People are seen barefoot in this century. A man carrying his dead young toddler son to cremate in his hometown. People carrying luggage and family on his shoulders. Unbelievable that these poor labourers were living right below your high rise apartments and no one noticed them. Now they are out in the open, running scared toward their homelands. The dirtiest thing is politics and politicking minds, even in such harsh, unliveable conditions too. When bellies are full, people belch out politics and religion. A mundane day is spent to enter a mundane night. Life without visions and the future.

Day 55

18 May 2020, Monday

The results of the first human tests of any COVID-19 vaccine are out, carried out first by Moderna, a US-based company, and are said to be in order, and satisfactory. It was injected in eight volunteers in the USA in March. The samples, when tested in the laboratory, gave a sufficient number of antibodies present the same as those in recovered patients of COVID-19 infection. There is no halt in cases rising in India. Only slightly less compared to yesterday's figure of five thousand two hundred and forty-two, today it was around four thousand five hundred. I used about with numbers as when I check after that it was rising too slightly. Absolutely no change in the atmosphere at all. Whichever day I write, it's the same. The day meets into the night. And night into day. It's an endless saga. For me at least, as I have no school from home or college from home, or work from home. I have no business to run. I am a seafarer and now that option is also bleak. I am in the middle of shifting to my new home, which is incomplete and still a few months away for us to shift. I had my own nice villa to live in till February 2020. I sold to go to a bigger house. But since that was not ready, I am on rent now at my current residence in an apartment. We never lived in an apartment. Coming from a small town, Rohtak, we had our comfort in independent houses only. Well, now we are stuck here with the excess burden of rent and shortening of earnings. This might be the story of many in big town Gurugram, which is the frontrunner at the moment in Haryana. I am scared to go back to my folks in Rohtak, as my parents are elderly and in their seventies. Corona has distanced families in a way.

Day 56

19 May 2020, Tuesday

It was yet another devastating day as far as per-day numbers are concerned in India; it has shot up past six thousand now. And India now has reached in top regions as far as per the total number of cases is concerned. On Sunday, one professor said that "Ashwagandha" boosts immunity; in India, it's a popular ayurvedic drug with no side effects. It has antiviral properties, too. "Withania Somnifera" is Ashwagandha, which literally means Ashwa (horse) and gandha (Smell); it means smelly like a horse.

IIT (D) Delhi said in a statement that the researchers targeted the main SARS CoV 2'5 enzyme to split proteins known as main protease, or Mpro. Mpro play a key role in mediating viral replication. This researcher found that Witananone (Wi-N), a natural compound derived from Ashwagandha and Catteic Acid Phenethyl Ester (CAPE), an ingredient found in New Zealand propolis, have the ability to block the activity of the Mpro. They said in the right quality, controlled resources and extracts must be used for particular effects. The total cases now in India are one hundred and six thousand four hundred and seventy-five: sixty thousand eight hundred and fifty-eight active, forty-two thousand three hundred and nine recovered, and three thousand three hundred and two deceased. The total in the world is nearing fifty lakhs today, at four million, nine hundred and sixty-six thousand one hundred and fifteen cases, with three hundred and twenty-three thousand six hundred and seventy-five deaths and one million, nine hundred and forty-nine thousand one hundred and ten recovered. World Bank has extended aid of one hundred and sixty billion dollars to one hundred nations. Worry is far from over.

Day 57

20 May 2020, Wednesday

The vaccine ChAdOx1 nCoV-19, an initiative by Oxford University, has failed to stop infection in monkeys. It's a severe blow to the scientists there and their performers, who were in process of manufacturing the same, including one 'Serum' based in Pune. A new Thailand-based company has also claimed a vaccine is being developed there. Now, Moderna, a US-based company, is the one with the promise of a successful vaccine in offering so far, by the code name mRNA–1273. The count remained with five thousand five hundred and forty-seven new cases added to India's COVID-19 count in twenty-four hours, making a total of one hundred and twelve thousand and twenty-eight new cases. By 25th May, partial opening of domestic air travel will be allowed. It's a tough situation for a nation choosing between death from hunger or death from COVID-19 coronavirus. Most nonessential markets remain to be shut. People remain indoors. People remain anxious. Partial lockdown is opening but life's normalcy remains paralyzed totally. International Hockey Federation has announced no matches till a viable vaccine is available. People remain in prayers and locked indoors.

Day 58

21 May 2020, Thursday

Now corona jokes have faded online. The musicians play out from balconies. The balcony parties are no longer fed on happening. Most are either frustrated being locked up or scared. Indiabulls are said to be relieving two thousand of its employees. The employees were sent notices on WhatsApp and emails and they lost their jobs, just like that. New Zealand's prime minister is suggesting a four-day week. New Zealand has already opened up. Now, most calls that I get from friends have one question only: will a cure come and how long will this situation of locked down last? Many have become irritable and have lost humour in such a crisis. I feel sad for the kids. They needed to be out playing and meeting friends, exploring the world, making new friends going to school, and playing games. But it is all not happening. The elderly population remains scared and doubtful. They are the ones watching T.V. the whole day and have maximum questions to ask. My mother updates her knowledge about corona daily, though we both are in different towns. She is in Rohtak and we are in Gurugram, but we talk daily over the phone. For their safety and fears, I am not going to meet them there. All families are like this, some locked in together. Others were locked out.

Day 59

Dreams; I had a word with some friends about a horrible dream that I had. I told them that the whole night, whenever I am closing my eyes and falling asleep, I see various symptoms of COVID-19 affecting me. Oh God, did I get it? Sweating, I would wake up and relax for a while before falling asleep again and it repeats. Sometimes there was the difficulty of breathing. Other times pulsating chest. At times, not breathing at all, I would wake up gasping for air and then gulping air in large volumes. Many of my friends have repetitive dreams. Some of the series they watch on the net, and others of monsters. But all have disturbed sleep patterns. It has induced a fear psychosis in people. I counter it by not watching the news. I check once only on the net. The confusion lingers on, debates rage on incessantly about lockdown effectiveness, herd immunity and the vaccine of coronavirus. We have knowledge about this disease through news channels. Where various doctors give their views at times, views are contradicting too. No one knows for sure what to do, except social distancing.

Washing hands, masks, sanitizer. The effectiveness of drugs. Symptoms, line of treatment, and recovery rates are all differently seen in different countries.

Day 60

What goes on in minds in life post-corona? E-commerce, E-governance, work from the home 4-day week. The working staff in offices shall be one fifth of strength and will be new normal. They will come to offices for meetings and planning twice or thrice a week. Maximum working days might be four days only in a week. Commercial buildings won't get leased out so easily. Lease rates will fall; long-term leases will be a thing of the past. Mortgage and loan seekers will drop. Fixed deposits and monthly returns schemes will prosper. Getaway homes will be a thing. People will socialize only with the known. Xenophobia shall rise. Migrations shall decrease, intra-country and intercontinental. The unorganised sector will get organised. Farming fisheries hatcheries, fishermen shall attract an educated lot. These sectors shall get organised too. The health industry will boom; preventive healthcare especially. Healthy lifestyles might be the norm. Insurance seekers might rise. The recreation and hotel industry will be hit. Shipping, aviation, too, shall get a hit. Carbon footprint will decrease. Farm and dairy produce shall get a thumbs up from big investors. Villages will be new small-scale industry hubs. All this is my vision as I lay in my bed thinking day and night.

Day 61

The numbers per day have gone up to seven thousand plus. Is it a maximum, or shall we see a new high again? Russia's cases per day have gone above ten thousand; USA is even up to thirty-two thousand in a day. The world is battered totally now. Disarrayed and in shock. Whosoever had any doubts that corona would not affect their country is no more disillusioned. Most countries, like Spain, the UK, Germany, Italy, China, and even the USA, had peaked between thirty to forty-five days or so. India's number keeps rising slowly but steadily. There is hardly any social distancing lift if practically seen. Most people have started socializing by now. Evening witnesses hordes of families out walking, only ten per cent in masks, in societies and sixty per cent out in markets. People have taken to drinking as a getaway from the tension of corona. There is absolutely no protection of the rights of citizens to live peacefully or live off lesser salaries. Court has dispelled any respite for tenants too on rent. From the lowest ring of society to the highest, all are hit.

Day 62

25 May 2020, Monday

From extremely pessimistic views that there will never ever be a vaccine for coronavirus to the very optimistic view that a coronavirus vaccine will be available by the end of the year, mankind is swinging like a pendulum emotionally. Those who go out to the office or for a sneaky socialize later in the night keep tossing in bed, wondering if they have contracted the ill-fated disease.

I just cannot get schoolkids out of my mind. They need to be outside playing, learning, meeting and finding what life is. I tell myself, "Each day passes by, bringing us closer to the end of the COVID-19 score" and perhaps a permanent solution too. Some Indian companies have joined the league of vaccine explorers. We might be six months behind the first one. But it's never too late.

Hope the coronavirus does not have second or third waves like the disastrous 1918 Spanish flu. WHO is rethinking on use of hydroxychloroquine for treatment. It's one of the only drugs found bit suitable to cure COVID-19. Many more companies have joined the hunt for coronavirus. Hope someone brings it around by the end of the year of 2020.

Day 63

26 May 2020, Tuesday

Total cases in the world so far: five million, six hundred and forty-eight thousand three hundred and forty-four. Deaths: three hundred and fifty thousand two hundred and eighty-seven. Recovered: two million, four hundred and nine thousand nine hundred and seven. India now has a total of one hundred and fifty thousand seven hundred and ninety-three cases: five thousand eight hundred and forty-three new cases added, four thousand three hundred and ninety-seven deaths so far and one hundred and twenty-one five hundred and seven recovered. The majority of migrant labourers have left by now from their workplaces. A few domestic air routes are opened. I am fed up writing the same story over and over for more than two months now. It's damn frustrating. A totally repetitive lifestyle, and the same patterns of days and nights. I wish to break free, but cannot.

Day 64

27 May 2020, Wednesday

Is WHO a fair body? An effective body? Many questions are already raised. Are drug manufacturers mafias? Hydroxychloroquine is being shot down by WHO; is there an influence of a single nation behind it, that wants to push its own more expensive drug in markets? We have the right to ask. And ask shall we always. Now there are rumors about Moderna's vaccine, too, floundering on its way, though my knowledge is from my net searches and WhatsApp forwards. Solid news on the vaccine is still elusive. COVID-19 is now accepted that it is all around us. Two main things have come out: washing or sanitizing hands and a distance of more than four feet that people try to follow, and masks when in markets and on walks. People try or are prepared to meet only known people from close circles. People had gone nuts; online, one car, sanitized inside and out, got burned in Delhi's scorching heat. Kerala, which had almost recovered and gone down to almost below twenty cases in total, now again has risen to about four hundred and fifty cases. COVID-19 is like a ghost. You don't know when it can appear.

Day 65

28 May 2020, Thursday

There are locked-down days that began unofficially about seventy days back and officially in India now sixty-five days continuously. Novavax has purchased the Indian company Serum institute, and they will continue making the product vaccine for COVID-19. Oxford, Moderna, Novavax, Sinovac, etc. are still in the hunt, along with Italian, German, and Thai, companies, for the vaccine. Many in the field of virology are still doubtful about a credible vaccine. But many are very optimistic too. Life thrives on hope. The Indian government's homeopathic department has advised taking Arsenicum-album-30 on an empty stomach first thing in the morning for two months, as per Ayush department too. Ayush is the Ayurvedic department. The scene is such that people are eating anything to survive, from lemon, ginger, Ayurvedic, and homeopathic medicines. Cases have never ceased to grow in numbers. India has not yet ceased.

17th September 2020, Thursday

I am on board at sea, sailing on MT Ardmore Sealifter, a ship owned by an Irish company named after perhaps the owner's hometown of "Ardmore", which means 'evermore'. I left home on the evening of 3rd Septemer and landed onboard on midnight of 5th Sept, going into 6th September. Almost four months have passed since I wrote last. There was not much to write. Corona has literally taken happiness out of mankind. By now, millions world over have lost jobs and much more are infected. It says to say how that disease has taken a form of a taboo now. People infected do get marginalized and strictly avoided, even after becoming negative. It was my nightmare to go do a COVID-19 test. I faced my ghosts and accepted the responsibility to relieve a fellow seafarer, chief engineer on his ship. He met an accident and got his leg sprained. Upon his request, I came forward and did my test, twice: once on 29th August and on 2nd September. Thankfully negative, hence I am here.

9th Nov 2020, Monday

The pen is such a thing that the ink freezes without warning. So did my pens for months.

11th November 2020, Wednesday

It's a race now, between my dwindling, fading, waning, glorious career at sea, the infamous year 2020, and corona, the sickest disease dread scare. I am on board Ardmore Sealifter now. Already two months have passed, and news of corona is none the rarer here at sea than a scare. It's been a real, most dreadful year at sea, for me, joining the ship, staying on board in my career spanning from 9th Feb 1996 till now. It has been going on for maybe two months more. I sit on the chief engineer's chair. A chair was reserved by me, where I sat in the year 2005. Most guys on this chair must have been better than me. I, I was only a by-chance engineer. Not very knowledgeable, rational, a survivor, and my prayer. God has been kind this far. It's been sixteen years as chief engineer and twenty-five years at sea. A lifetime of a career. I am tired, too, but not so old. I am looking back at the land with respect to take me back where I was born.

12th November 2020, Thursday

Days keep progressing, and so does corona. It has stayed the test of time and people's health resistance. This would probably go down as the biggest worldwide happening of our generation. Europe is under another lockdown already. Only trickles of news at the moment. Formal and effective vaccines yet to take shape. Here now, I watch all from afar, from the ship hich appears safe. But many other ship's crew too had infections. It's such a year for me. I sold my house, moved to rent, left the rented accommodation, and moved to a new house. Only my family moved in. I moved in to ship for this last remaining journey, the voyage at the fag end of my career. October tormented my sail due to a series of mishaps on board and an oil overflow from tanks onto the deck, which could have culminated into a major thing had it been overboard, but luckily not. That, too, in crossing the English Channel on 16th October.

16th November 2020, Monday

No news of effective mass vaccination as yet, either from Sputnik 'V', or Oxford vaccine, or Indian Covaxin, or Chinese Sinovac, or Moderna. The world is weary and tired of waiting. Countries tried lockdown, then opening up, and again lockdown; results are more or less persistent. The corona has stayed here unstopped, except for a few island nations like New Zealand, Australia, etc. The rest are all gripped by corona till today. I am still onboard, now sailing from Antwerp to a Moroccan port, carrying diesel in a product tanker. Life is aggrieved on board of non-timely reliefs, no more leaves, and unabated job pressures, which are now remotely controlled by these managers sitting in Singapore, Hong Kong, Dubai, etc. Some guys get to stay at home and work from home, sailors no they are not. It is deemed safe for their travellers to join ships but unsafe to go out of there. Corona has lashed up all backs equally.

26th November 2020, Thursday

Drifting off Gibraltar. Corona runs unabated in the world. There has been a third lockdown of Europe and Asian countries. Christmas is going to come and pass, the same as Diwali did, in fear and hope. Rounds of cold chains to support the delivery of vaccines is talked about now. Runners-up above are Pfizer, Moderna, Sputnik V, Covaxin, Sinovac, and AstraZeneca. Talks to vaccinate citizens have begun, with results of vaccines as low as seventy to ninety-two per cent seems good. Yet to see results on the grand scale of en masse vaccination. On ships, we battle loneliness, thoughts of the making of safety and perils of sea and other things, but hope keeps us all going, whether at sea, air, land, or up above in the universe. I write sitting in the chief engineer's chair of merchant tanker Ardmore Sealifter. May God have mercy.

28th November 2020, Saturday

Oxford vaccine thinks to back off now, due to mixed results of the third stage trials: up to seventy per cent effective. Meanwhile, about a million farmers from Punjab and Haryana have marched to the Indian capital Delhi from as far as four hundred km, and have swarmed Delhi for their demands to roll back an agro bill recently passed by Govt. It's strange to see people risk everything for their rights. I see it as a positive ray of hope. Corona will get beaten and many farmers will win their rightful demands. Meanwhile, on the ship, we are drifting off Gibraltar. Vessels are normally safer, with no infections on board. Here, more concerns are for their sign-offs, for food, water, and sleep. Life exists in all faces: at sea, on land, as farmers, sailors, and all want to live honourably and peacefully. May corona close, may sailors be at peace, may farmers be at peace. I keep tracking hope. I get to write a suitable vaccine's triumph one day. Good night.

29th November 2020, Sunday

The world probably now stands at crossroads. Cleaner energy is definitely the way forward. Nations will aggressively look to cut carbon footprints. Air pollution will be brought down to zero. Maybe COVID-19 was, is, a signal. AstraZeneca seems to be backing off their vaccine. But many are still in the queue. Hope is in the air. Hope is the essence of life. It has kept people, industries, nations going so far in 2020. December knocks soon. All feel that January 2021 may usher in changing times. The world will heal, and get out of the misery of corona. Sailors, too, await good news, as now they cannot step down gangways. The only time signing on or signing off is when they land ashore. They are onto the challenge and grinding it out at sea; it's business as usual.

12ᵗʰ December 2020, Saturday

I returned back from my vessel about a month earlier than expected. It was a gruelling contract of three months, a series of happenings keeping me on edge. An almost oil spill in the English Channel could have landed me in sure trouble, even jail maybe. But luckily nothing went overboard. Though the matter was reported to Jouborg French port authorities, who reverted by saying it falls into English jurisdiction. But then the matter went silent. The company was satisfied by all records not pointing to an oil spill. This, followed by steering gear failure, and complete boiler plant failure, led me as chief engineer and my fellow engineers, Rohan, Gupte, Atul Pandey, and Bharthry, into dismay and fear. Work was almost round the clock. I couldn't write much on board because of a seriously busy tenure. The fizz of joining the vessel and signing off was taken off by a series of corona tests. Twice, swab tests from the nasal passages prior to joining the vessel. Again, in Santos, Brazil, a blood test was done. Upon sign off, a swab test from the mouth at Gibraltar. There is always an anxiety in waiting for test results. Luckily, so far so good. London Heathrow was so deserted both times in September as well as in December as I transited through it both times. It's strange we do not see faces any more. Shopkeepers, air hostesses, ground staff, pilots, seamen flying in, and others – all are masked at all times. British Airway was my flyer from Delhi to London and London to Santos when joining the ship in September. I left the vessel by a small boat and arrived at a hotel in Gibraltar,

Holiday Inn, overlooking a big, well-maintained Christian cemetery sandwiched between the airport and hotel. My window opened daily to salute the dead first and begin the day. Then British Airways flew me from Gibraltar to London, and London to Delhi.

In-flight, you wear masks and a face shield of plastic with a headband wrapped around your head to keep it fixed at all times. In three-row seats, the poor middle-seat person will have a wear a gown too, in addition. Luckily, I had an aisle seat, so some consolation. The cases of corona are dropping sharply now in India, with an almost ninety-seven per cent recovery rate. Some encouraging signs. The day the first official jab of the Pfizer vaccine was given in London, I was there at the airport. NHS has initiated the process of vaccination. The UK is first country to approve. It was Tuesday, 8th December 2020. Looks like corona's days have begun a reverse countdown now. Phew, what a year 2020 is.

14th December 2020, Monday

I maintained a streak of continuous writing initially. Then job daily chores got the better of me, and intermittent writing started. Now Pfizer shots are given in the UK and a report of facial palsy has surfaced as a side effect. People at this juncture are both sceptical as well as optimistic about various vaccines. Of all now, Pfizer is leading, along with Russian Sputnik V. Oxford AstraZeneca is on the heels, and Chinese Sinovac is too. Indian vaccine Covaxin is about a month behind the leader. Most vaccines are suggesting a second shot after about fifteen days. God knows if it will be a mass experiment of the world or a mass cure, or prevention. More than fifty per cent of world doses of vaccine will be in joint ventures with Indian Pharma companies, which produce as well as research on viral infections. Serum Institute is the leading producer of the corona vaccine at the moment. I am in my new home now, post sign-off from the ship. It's beautiful. Balconies open into backyard park. It's an open, airy villa of about five thousand five hundred square feet, with a lift in it.

This is the first in my life, the seeing of the corona pandemic. As said earlier, I had to undergo tests for corona four times due to flying out of India and joining the ship and then back to home. Things changed now since I began writing in March. The world has opened up more. So have markets, bazaars, and people. There is an air of optimism in the air. Vaccines have arrived. Perhaps humanity will survive another epidemic. We were here to see it.

We witnessed these days. Days of loneliness, lockdowns, and at times people sleeping hungry. Life had come to a grinding halt. But life goes on. Once again it will. I am penning off now. I wish the world recovers from the novel coronavirus.

I will go on a world tour by road someday, without a mask, and hug and shake hands with strangers. Yes, it was a year no one would want to recall. A year minus happy memories. The year 2020. 2020 is the invisible year.

There was an absolute lull of time, and I am writing now after a long gap, but writing nevertheless. This (COVID-19) now appears to be another version of the flu, with its newer protocol of medication and testing. I have had it twice, with all symptoms mostly, sore throat, tiredness, fever (at times high fever). Once it lasted only four days. I had it on 29th March 2022. And then for about eleven to twelve days: mild fever, sore throat, cough, tiredness, dripping nose. The shorter duration had a higher fever. Almost all of my known have had it by now. It is not a taboo any more. But the way it infects people is strange. When I had the first infection, I did not transmit it to anyone at home. Crowded rooms, no masks. But the second time I had already joined ship, and perhaps a newly joined crew in England spread it to all. Poor third engineer got it too, who was relieved and had to be quarantined for fifteen days in the UK prior to going to his home after six months at sea. Later, the whole crew got it.

12th July 2022, Tuesday

At the port of TUXPAN Mexico, outer anchorage. Suddenly, on the vessel's PA system, it is announced, "All come to the ship's office for temperature check." All are expecting at least a female doctor coming on the ship to do COVID tests, which are mandatory nowadays. There was one, but she was wearing a mask, and we, too, were in masks, giving away our temperature to her for free, but hiding excitement behind masks. It was over in a few minutes, all twenty-two crew checked, all healthy. mockery of COVID tests and COVID is such, seafarers are deprived of their rights of shore leave. But visitors can visit their ship, and may even infect them. World over, cases rises and fall. COVID now is no more than a bar graph or a sinusoidal curve of rising and falling cases. Boris Johnson has resigned. But Queen Elizabeth shall never relinquish her divine right to the throne of the British Empire – poor Charles. Anyway, they, too, had COVID and are fine now. The vessel is firmly anchored off the TUXPAN.

13th July 2022, Wednesday

It's warm – thirty-two degrees Celsius, Gulf of Mexico. Anchored off the TUXPAN port still. This write-up has mostly been about COVID-19. But also, times during the pandemic. Every month, Mexico is revising its policy of allowing seafarers for shore leave. It's July 2022, and this month no shore leave here. But you can see the port of TUXPAN from afar. Many more merchant tankers are anchored here. Smoke billowed out from the chimneys of the port facility and refineries. Cranes are always sighted from distance. There is a small swimming pool on board. All take a dip in it after post-day work. It's painted blue from the inside and has signs around reading, "Caution: slippery area" and "No diving." But some did dive into it a few days back. Now, we only swim.

17th July 2022, Sunday

The vessel remains at anchor. It's Sunday, but now there is news of going to SBM for discharging at eight p.m. It's quarter to five p.m. now. Soon, engine room will receive a notice at one hour to prepare engines to take her to sea buoy mooring operations, where floating cargo pipelines are waiting to join the ship's discharge manifold pipes, to let her discharge her cargo of ultra-low sulphur diesel. Cases in India are twenty thousand plus per day. The news of swine flu, SARS virus, and monkeypox virus keep doing rounds on the internet, which is a major source of news on the ship, as there is no TV here. Cases have not vanished anywhere in any country so far. Corona as yet remains a pandemic. My wife, daughter, and son have recently recovered from COVID, and the dripping of nose and throat congestion linger on for up to a month. We at sea perhaps recover faster, maybe due to unpolluted air, exercises, fixed time for meals, maybe a mind more occupied with assignments of various jobs on a daily basis. War knows no pandemic, it in itself is one. The Russo-Ukraine war has raged on now for many months already. Many thousands were killed. Humans just wish to perish with one pandemic or another.

23rd July 2022, Saturday

Now finally berthed at the port of TUXPAN, after a long time at anchorages and SBMs. As expected, there is no shore leave, and if at all there, you have to undergo an RTPCR test when coming back. It's such a hassle. By now, all know the unreliability of these tests. Many have narrated false test reports. And suppose you are negative, no problem, you come back on ship and continue. But if positive, your contract will be terminated. No one risks that. Strange is the case of this pandemic. The world is open yet closed. Selective openings. Surveyors and pilots can board a vessel, but not vice versa. A ship whose crew is at sea and in isolation is a threat, whereas persons boarding the ship are not. It appears the saga of corona will either be for couple more years, or it will be like the common flu. Time only will tell. Prince George of English royalty posed with the Wimbledon trophy, holding it, and Djoker grinning next to him, the real winner of this trophy this year. Djoker did not vaccinate himself and missed out on the Australian Open. But then he is Djoker, the great Djokovic. Prince George, the future King of England seems from London.

26th July 2022, Tuesday

Still at TUXPAN, discharging diesel via the ship's pipeline to shore trucks. Almost all port workers wear masks. The trucks line up at the loading manifold junction. Drivers keep chatting with each other. We watch from the vessel's decks. A few wanted to go out; in fact, all wanted. None could, as no shore leave is permitted due to corona. About three officers wanted to see a doctor for a nose boil, ear wax, and another with a scratchy itch on the palm, which was injury from job only on ship. Agent was contacted and a doctor's visit was arranged, instead of letting men go to the doctor, to the disappointment of the sailor patients, who wanted to go out. The doctor visited, perhaps not welcomed much, got furious and the next day came with two more doctors. They took samples of tissue with swabs from the skin near the ear, nose, and palm. We discussed this in the meeting. All now on-board wear masks, as doctors are there. No one knew why tissue swabs were taken for ear wax. Finally, the mail came from the shore health officer; it was the test protocol for monkeypox. A new menace trying to emerge.

28th July 2022, Thursday

TUXPAN still it is. No results yet for three tested for monkeypox. The chief cook lost his father, for the heavenly abode he left. Poor Job Daniel had applied for his relief a month back. But alas, to make things worse, a five-day embargo on not letting down the ship's gangway till monkey pox results are out. These three men are asked to be in quarantine, and for no reason, they are fine. Such are Mock the monkey, typ of games played nowadays. Even my reliever is in a hotel along with the chief cook. I am the chief engineer of this ship, Hafnia Phoenix. And my reliever and new chief cook will be subjected to a COVID test on 3rd August. In all likelihood, I may leave this vessel by the 5th or 6th. The job may go on dispensation sign-off by 31st July or 1st August, without a reliever. Just to catch up with the world, new vaccines are available for even toddlers. Almost sixty per cent of world has been doubly vaccinated. Yet almost all those who were vaccinated had COVID, including me twice. It appears it might go away by next year's end, just my hunch. The discharging rate is very slow here, due to unloading by trucks. The vessel might be here till 9th August. I shall be gone from the vessel hopefully by then. Commonwealth Games have kicked off in Birmingham, UK. All pomp and show and thousands of athletes from Commonwealth Countries. Apart from sports nothing else is common in Common Wealth countries.

29th July 2022, Friday

At last, Job Daniel, the chief cook, gets to go home. Mexican Port authorities and health authorities permitted him as a case of emergency. He will disembark the ship around midnight. Last night, through a video call from a friend's borrowed net, he saw his father's last rites, his burial, as he was Christian. Job still cooked the dinner today. That sums up the spirit of sailors. He would always smile whenever I used to meet him, apart from the last two days. He is not going to do an RTPCR test for COVID, as the airlines don't need it. He will be given a taxi ride to Mexico City, a drive of more than an hour from TUXPAN. Then till ten a.m. on 30th July, he will wait at the airport on some lonely bench alone. I, meanwhile, am still waiting for me to go; it might be when a reliever who is putting up in a hotel finishes his COVID test, plus forty-eight hours more after 3rd August. I reckon 6th. I might get to go too. The health authorities still have not sent the monkey pox sample analysis report; that too might be around 3rd August. And till then, no one embarks or disembarks this ship, a tanker of about fifty thousand tonnes carrying ULSP, a form of diesel. Life is mundane on ships nowadays. No shore leaves at times and COVID tests, isolation. Plus working hours, which mostly exceed thirteen hours in a day. In the night, we retire back to cabins to watch movies or some series. People watch in their free time. Luckily, my cabin is big, with a computer and a big TV too.

30th July 2022, Saturday

So, finally, cook Job Daniel left the vessel around nine p.m., LT TUXPAN, Mexico. Most of the crew turned up to say bye to him till gangway. After all, cooks are mothers of ships, they feed us. Job left with drooped shoulders and no smile, ever smiling Job. He didn't turn back or wave back. Sad circumstances to leave a ship. A father who must have been proud to see him going on ship, on Job's first ship – now Job will never meet him, never. I am also counting days now; it might be the 6th or 7th when I leave vessel too. The end days of the contract are the most anxious. You are on edge to leave duties and head home. Above all, you are tired at sea. Cases keep rising and falling around the globe with this continuous dreadful, life-altering curse of COVID. God only knows when it will finally go. In the name of COVID tests, rackets have started around holding travellers till they bribe and go out. Hotels, too, have devised strategies to get customers to test positive and retain them for weeks in the name of quarantines. Now, orders from the company have forbidden the usage of alcohol on board, though it was only beers, but now no more. Strangely, the decision to bar alcohol on board is taken by people who straight away head to bars after meetings, or come from bars to take decisions. Alas, poor sailors. Cases have risen in Delhi since yesterday now to almost one thousand five hundred a day. There seems no lift up from COVID till now. There is no cook on board now. Only Steward Rao makes up for Job.

31st July 2022, Sunday

Is it a season, an era of pandemics, wars, or economic destruction? Much of the world is already ravaged by the combined effects of COVID-19, and the Russo-Ukrainian War. And then the economy got toppled worldwide. Sri Lanka's president has fled the nation, and people have stormed the palace of the president in Lanka. Pakistan may collapse, if not already. APKR is now 270 worth a single USD. Cases of COVID in India are about nineteen thousand plus in a single day, which is perhaps a new normal. Most people have stopped reporting COVID cases and treat themselves at home only. Severe breathlessness perhaps is now gone from COVID symptoms. People are learning to live with it. Indians are now the new globe trotters. CWG has progressed today to number three in the UK. Here on board, I eagerly await my relief and head back home. Relief is that I will not be subjected to a COVID test in Mexico and will be flown straight to India by Indirect flights. A COVID Vaccinated Certificate is enough to carry and pass-through channels at airports, hotels, resorts, and pools. The travel world is opened back. A few back months, I was in Amsterdam, and the streets were flooded, a stampede-like situation. Streets smelled of beer, alcohol, smoke, prostitutes and pimps, and tourists too, but no smell of corona anywhere.

1st August 2022, Monday

And now, now there is the biggest twist in the story so far. All three officers tested, and two were declared positive for monkeypox and for one chickenpox. Yes, you heard it right: chickenpox too. I had so far only heard of Mafia. It is my first time seeing it. Mail has come to the vessel. So, we don't know what unfolds next. Tomorrow daytime will see a flurry of mail to and from the ship. The officers tested, yes, they are shit-scared of losing their jobs. The vessel might be quarantined for fourteen days further. My reliever is in the hotel in TUXPAN City; what will happen to my relief or his joining? Time only can tell. Job the cook finally reached his hometown in Kerala in India, and is grieving his father's loss with his kin. In the night, it's tense out here. Any daily show of Queen of South is on hold till I resume after writing. Seafarers were always the weakest, unprotected lot, at the mercy of port owners, charterers, and companies who hired them. Today, no talk of corona, only monkeypox and chickenpox. Sailors on board are trying to laugh it off, as if a joke. The joke it is. Tomorrow, I come back with more progress in the hot matter.

3rd August 2022, Wednesday

And in the monkey-gate, oops, in the monkeypox saga, the Mexicans suggested fumigating the ship, at the cost of about eight thousand USD, despite Master's protest that the vessel was already done upon arrival on 12th July. The reports sent bore different dates of "sample was taken on", "feche de toma", as reports were in Spanish. The vessel protested that dates and reports appear to be fake, and the reply from Health & Port administration, simply said, "very sorry", dates got mixed up. So, they maintained their stance of keeping vessel and so-called affected officers in quarantine. Now, Health officially again visited and checked all twenty-one crew on board. A visual inspection of the chest and back, with a little finger of the female doctor trying to find moles on the body. All inspected by the lady report escaped. They tried to mark down one engineer, who was bitten by mosquitos, as a suspect. But luckily, all this time were spared. And my reliever and cook now are cleared to join the vessel, on the master's, charterers, and owner's guarantee of taking responsibility for incoming relievers.

Cook Job had already left, but I cannot get down in Mexico, TUXPAN. So, my reliever sails on with me. Now, we go to the anchored pilot, who agreed to take us there. Immigration will clear remotely. The hotel made many. Perhaps fumigators, too, will reach eight a.m. We are again at anchor till the 9th in quarantine and then we will sail to a likely US load port through the Gulf of Mexico. Corona has taken a back seat now. I'd rather go back to my regular stories, binge-watching, and catch up later. It's nine p.m. at night already. I managed to walk for three hours and hit the bed then.

04th August 2022, Thursday

TUXPAN, the port that will go down in memory and love, due to nothing else but monkeypox. My reliever and cook are finally allowed to board the vessel by tomorrow daytime, that is 5th of August, after a rapid antigen test for COVID. Once they get negative results, they can board. And me, well, I do not get to disembark. I shall sail on till a US port next loading. The whole day ding dong of messages kept happening between ship agents and local authorities. Finally, post the eight thousand USD fumigation of the vessel, we shall leave the port of the TUXPAN, Denex terminal. Now, it's Houston for orders not yet confirmed. That means I stick around this ship for a week more. Here, it's business as usual on board. A hydraulic line leaked on the main dock. The second engineer and fitter, Arnold from the Philippines, repaired it. Second engineer, Praveen Sawan, myself, electrical officer, Shizo, and third engineer, Ankit Negi, are from India, and the crew in the engine room, fitter, Arnold, motorman, Randy, and wiper, John, are from the Philippines. We are a solid team. Engineers all smoke together. Like most engine rooms, this one too is hot and remains more so due to a vent supply out of order. COVID is on rise once more in Delhi and India. It just refuses to die down. But by now, medicines, precaution, and life is back to mostly normal.

5th August 2022, Friday

Left the port of TUXPAN and Pemex terminal by 1800 LT. My reliever and the cook did make it on time. The vessel has now sailed out towards Houston at about ten knots and main engine RPM at ninety-five. Both joiners had a negative COVID antigen test. These COVID tests are also a source of income for labs, doctors, agents, drugstores, hotels, and more, so a source that could or has fallen in hands of the Mafia. It is now a driving wheel for money making. Many unsuspected travellers are falling prey to it. In Birmingham, CWG India struck some gold in wrestling. Cases are unabatedly on a rise in India still. Corboevx, if I have the name correct, is another vaccine on the Indian scene. Ships, despite being the safest, are falling to COVID regularly. The world has, yes, positively changed post-COVID. And changes are that people are travelling with a vengeance. The economy has toppled. Handshakes with strangers are a no-no. Namaste, knuckle fists bumping is in. People have realised the value of freedom and health. Even the environment and hygiene too. Monkeypox is trying to emerge as a new epidemic. What times are these? Russians and Ukrainians are fighting for territory control. Sri Lanka is a broken economy. India has elected a new, tribal female president, Madam Droupadi Murmu.

7th August 2022, Sunday

We are adrift in non-ECA waters of the Gulf of Mexico. Right now, there are no orders to proceed. It likely is Houston. The monkeypox-gate got blown way out of proportion, and it surfaced in a local news network on TV and in local newspapers. The vessel and crew unnecessarily got famous for the wrong reason. There was no monkeypox to anyone. All are just working fine, no fever, no medicines, nothing. I am waiting to hear news of the vessel's plans to load. My sign-off will depend on it. Tomorrow, I should be hearing it from mails. I don't know how earlier pandemics ended, but corona looks like it is not leaving, even though three years already have elapsed. This certainly is one of the worst phases in the current fifty years of history that is known. Wars, economic turmoil, nations on edge threatening each other. China hates Nancy Pelosi's visit to Taiwan. It appears right is right has always prevailed and will go on. Bangladesh's fuel prices are doubled. The Pak rupee is getting crushed. Ukraine may be wiped out from the world map. But beacon hopes in sports continue in Birmingham. India stands in fourth position today. Indian wrestlers have raised gold by reigning on the mat. A COVID-positive Aussie cricketer was allowed to play in a mask against India.

8th August 2022, Monday

In the evening, post-dinner at my mandatory time of six p.m. to seven p.m., I went on the forecastle deck for an evening stroll, along with the vessel's Elec Shizo. A family of three fishes, what appeared to be a mother and two kids, blue, yellow, and green in colour, were swimming merrily from port side to starboard, at the bulbous bow. We discussed how beautiful sailing was in port. Boats will come to ships to take you to shore, no shore pass is needed. We would carry passports or any other identity. And now the vessel has news that shore leaves will be obtained by filling risk assessment forms and only to ports that do not carry out rapid antigen COVID tests. Once again, sailors lost out much more than civilians. The way things have happened in COVID, and the monkeypox era, not many will turn to seas. It's only dire need of a dime that makes one come out at sea, risking everything. I hope the world clock is turned fifty years back and we live more peacefully.

9th August 2022, Tuesday

As we drift, the vessel at times drifts too close to land. Drifting is a vessel, without using its engines, behaving as per the ocean's currents and wind force. We drifted closer to land, so had to use ship's engines to move away from it. We have been having issues with one of the main engine's six units. Unit No. 03 has had a knocking sound, a metallic knock. We change both the injection mounted on the cylinder head and the only exhaust valve tester, as the sound persists later. Today, after a brief lull, it again started and didn't go at any high or low RPMs at the engine. We have narrowed the root cause to the fuel pump; maybe a puncture, and the suction valves are leaking. We need to renew tomorrow morning's vessel. Super is also anxious and both I and relieving CE too are on edge. Hope it works out. In the long run, the cylinder liner has to be changed too, due to excessive iron content in scrape down analysis. We wait till tomorrow. I may hand over the charge tomorrow. Hope all goes well. COVID doesn't fade as old news, it's still the hottest talk. Hope this goes away this year. The vessel's itinerary is not fixed. I may go home from USA Corpus Christi, Houston; let's see. These are horrifying findings for engineers. A hell of a lot of unexpected jobs are now in hand. I left my cabin and have moved to a quieter cabin, the owner's cabin. Chief engineer's cabin is perhaps the most tensed on board: all technical matters last stoppage. I await my sign-off now. No news still of the next loading, we still drift. Whether we change liner before or after remains a huge question. Not sure if

I will sign off now in the US or later. But I am relieved. Ship's life has as little fun as a smoke-in tea break. Nowadays, most are glued to tablets, PCs, and laptops. I don't have any, never bought them. I have a not-so-advanced phone, but can be tuned to social media. Tomorrow will be a new day.

10th August 2022, Wednesday

I have handed over the charge of chief engineer of Hafnia Phoenix to my reliever. The No. 3 unit remains as it was. The latest attempt to work on fuel PIP SUC and Puncture VIV of MAN BEW 6SMCC has failed. After trying, knocking kept on in Unit No. 3. The pics later of the liner and ring pack of the piston revealed that the piston crown touches the liner walls. Now we will have to renew the liner, and the piston as well. The ball is in the office's court. We find high cat fines for silica & aluminium high in the bunker fuel in use, but the question remains why only the No. 3 unit, why not others, and, why now after more than thirty days of usage of the same fuel? We did a trans-Atlantic voyage from Amsterdam to New Orleans. Why now? We have switched to the last bunkered fuel, the ULSFO from New Orleans.

11th August 2022, Thursday

Still drifting in the non-ECA region of the Gulf of Mexico. The world still reels under COVID, and traces of monkeypox have started to spread. God forbid it becomes yet another pandemic. Life on board is like a different kind of world. Cut off from land. At sea, sea birds, too, are a rare sight, not even fish. Mermaids are folklore; I did not see one even close to them in the last twenty-six years at sea. What I noticed is a dwindling population of birds and fish. Increase in restrictions on seafarers. Stagnant salaries. Blame game culture is now part of the industry. Owners seldom know the true picture on board, the middle managers fool them by saying all is well. Crew welfare is at bottom of the priority list. There is a rare shore leave. Zero alcohol on board. You cannot go to shore and come back drunk. There are virtually zero parties now. Smoke rooms and mess rooms witness low attendance. Sailors are hooked to the unreal world of the net via tablets and laptops. The crew has longer contracts than officers and lower salaries. Master is merely a postman now, and a puppet, along with other ranks of ship. Most times, even basic medicines are missing from the ship's medical locker. Radio advice has taken place of real doctor visits. Cost cutting has killed even the frills and thrills of joining and signing off. I await my ticket back home, but merrily now, retired to the owner's cabin. I am now a passenger on the same ship where I was a chief engineer.

12th August 2022, Friday

This has become a long drifting period. In the evening walks to the fore castle deck, I regularly see a mother fish with a blue body and fins and yellow marks on the fins, with two kids of hers. Many others have seen her too. It has a flat round snout and fairly long body. It had rained today, and it was pleasant. The air isn't humid, but wet and cold. The week has come to a halt and the weekend has started. 15th August is Indian Independence Day. If we will stay in international waters, we shall hoist the tricolour, the Indian flag, and salute with the Indian national anthem. We shall feel proud then. It's a day in anticipation now. Since I have moved to this cabin, I do not have the ship's net on my desktop, which was faster. Now on my cell phone, I barely make one WhatsApp call with interruption to my wife and to mother. Almost no one calls me back. Sailors mostly have a giving relationship, as perhaps distances and time lets most on land forget them, or at least get used to their absence. I don't have much news on international affairs for the past three days. I tried to use one old lying TV, and fixed it with the help of fitter Arnold and Verky, but it does not have a remote, so I could not watch by my USB. I watch some clips on my phone at times. It's night, ten p.m. Life is slow here. Maybe Monday will have some news. I pen off now – not keen to write much today.

13th August 2022, Saturday

Actually, I had set off writing about the COVID pandemic when I first sat down with my pencil and paper. But the pencil took over, and I kept writing, drifting like my ship nowadays. I am writing the account of days now, as they came and went like passing waves. We used engines again to come back to our drifting coordinates. No. 3 unit still knocks when the main engine runs. We are gradually narrowing down now to fix the fault along the lines of high cat fines in bunker fuel oil. The fuel used is VLSFO: very low sulphur fuel oil. The cat fine is a fine metal particle of aluminium and silica, which are used in the fractional distillation process of crudes to turn it into usable fuel. They are such fine metal particles that they escape all filtering processes and all purification processes on board and even pass-through fuel pumps and fuel nozzles. Finally, they wear down the liner and fuel equipment. They did just that to the MAN B & W 6 SMCC engine of this fifty thousand ton chemical tanker. In the No. 3 unit, the piston now knocks at the piston cleaning ring and perhaps even slaps at the cylinder liner. So, that bad forty-two-high cat fine fuel bunkered at Amsterdam is now cut off, and we switched to other bunker tanks filled at New Orleans with lesser cat fines. The engine would run with noise but the damage is contained and the other units saved. And now we wait for company instructions on whether to do unit No.3 overhaul now or later.

14th August 2022, Sunday

Today is Pakistan's Independence Day. Good wishes to that brother nation too. And tomorrow is India's too. The preparations are afoot for some sweets and snacks prepared by the cook. Officers crew all are readying their white shirts, epaulets, black trousers, and shoes are being shined and shirts ironed. We are still drifting in the Gulf of Mexico, international water. So we can hoist the tricolour, the Indian national flag, too tomorrow, and the national anthem shall be sung along with it. I am in the cabin, now off all duties and waiting for the next news bringing loading information and details of my flight back to my motherland India. I am running into my fifth month now, almost midway. The sea remains blue, as it always is. The sky remains dark and light blue. No matter how many times you gaze at the night sky, it always mesmerizes one. I have already readied my uniform with epaulets tucked in flaps on my shoulders. On board, time remains slow when you are not part of the vessel's daily duties. I am counting the hours now for the next news. I have been long at sea, since 1996 Feb. This has been my bread and butter. This particular contract earnings will go to the education of my daughter, Varalika, who will do her master's in Law at King's College London. COVID is now fourteen thousand plus cases in India a day. Russia is still pounding Ukraine with its might. Ukraine is on slippery ground, steadily losing territory to the Russians, but not without a fight. The world merely watches on helplessly. Rakesh Jhunjhunwala, an Indian business tycoon, passed away at age of sixty-two, leaving humongous wealth to the mortal world. Life is only a counted number of days on Earth.

15th August 2022, Monday

Today was the 15th of August, Indian Independence Day. It was celebrated fittingly on board with the unfurling of the tricolour, followed by jalebis and samosas and ritualistic photographs, which lasted about one and a half hours. The Indian flag fluttered unhindered in the Gulf of Mexico. The captain had arranged all so well. It does give you a festival to celebrate on the ship. The vessel remains at mercy of the weather and waves, drifting. It's almost ten days now that we have still been drifting, without any orders. I am a passenger now on board. Let's see if tomorrow brings any news. COVID cases see a dip in India. Electric vehicles are catching up like wildfire all across the globe, a new revolution in the automobile industry. Not much mention of monkeypox in the news around the world, but due to the COVID pandemic already on, all nations have advisories for citizens and travellers on board. It's all normal so far. The crew are eager to step ashore in the US now, whenever the ship makes port. My last outing was more than forty days back, in Amsterdam. Shore leaves are a reprieve, a breather from the ship's hard life. Many companies and countries have stopped sailors nowadays from stepping foot ashore. Alcohol, too, is banned on ships. And now we cannot even come drunk from shore leaves. So, ships are a real sail now. This will see most sailors dropping out of this career. Poorer nations will step in with their sailors to fill in. And eventually, unnamed ships are going to be a reality of the future. I will wait for tomorrow if any schedule comes for the ship. Due to the imposing behaviour of visiting officially, Europe is least liked to be visited. America is still considered as being fair and square. Asian and African continents are dreaded, due to bribery and the unpredictability of port officials. Africa is still okay, as at least post the bribes, the vessels are not disturbed much. Recently, in a post state inspection, the vessel staff, especially the engineer, were unnecessarily heckled by legal administration, and many unnecessary defects were flagged, as they were not duly bribed. That was at San Lorenzo. It's an open secret of ships that they have to indulge in corruption or bribery or else face the music of delays and fines and sanctions. Now even COVID & monkeypox havoc become tools for earning, as was in TUXPAN.

16th August 2022, Tuesday

There is news now that the vessel's next voyage might be fixed: loading ULSD from Houston, Texas, USA, and discharging in Brazil, though the voyage shall be confirmed only the day after tomorrow; that is, by the 18th. Looks like my countdown to go home will get confirmed only past the 18th. So, that is more like it as of now. The major repairs on main engine might be done at a lay-up berth in Houston, likely post-loading. Serum Institute claims to have developed a very effective vaccine for COVID 19, especially for the Omicron variant. The crew on board is excited about the prospective Brazil voyage. Sailors always love South America more, and Brazil the most, for their free culture, free of radicalization of races, colour, or economic superiorities.

17th August 2022, Wednesday

The thing about being on ships is loneliness and stress. There are two things that do not leave a sailor. For engineers, a call to the cabin is always an emergency or job or something that calls for attention – mostly immediate attention. And at sea, you cannot ignore it, and there is no help. You are the help to the whole ship. This certainly induces stress, and that's why you need relief in time. COVID has tested sailors' limits. On my ship, a few are running into the tenth month of their stretch. Even I, into my fifth month and despite a reliever on board, am not relieved until I disembark. I still wait for news of that. Tomorrow, it might come. Meanwhile, I write, play TT, go for walks, and go to the engine room. But now I am an intrusion to working staff. And for about eighteen hours of the day, I stand mostly locked in this cabin. The news that I follow is the Ukraine-Russia war, the COVID situation, and Indian news. Limited access is available here, which sometimes on other ships is not the case. The hours witness me just passing time sitting idle for hours, tossing in bed. Sleep is a luxury on board. Deep sleep, no, it never is. But you just rest your body. Food has become recreation, so you long to go to the mess room, and if it's good, it's a real treat.

18th August 2022, Thursday

See, patience is the name of the game if you are ever born in your next life as a sailor. You must patiently work. Patiently wait for your turn to go back home. And those who are born to sail this life would have maximum hope for a luxury cruise as a passenger. Well, now, still no news if we get to berth for loading by this weekend, or if will it be next week. There is an absolute lull about COVID or monkeypox on board. I think that none talk about it any more. Unfortunately, the same is the case of the Russo-Ukraine War. But we are hearing now that three Ukrainians are joining this vessel in the USA, along with a hydro blaster, a machine used for deck maintenance. Good that at least some of them are still getting employment. In drifting, a vessel abides by fixed coordinates. If it drifts further away from the limit, the vessel's engines are used to come back to those coordinates only. Apart from a few games of chess, a few rounds of smoke, a game of TT, and some gym enthusiasts, there is not much now. The alleyways are silent, and so are other common areas. Without alcohol, there are no parties on board. And now there is absolutely none here. The company is trying to ban it totally. Though, I heard a few good ones in Denmark are trying in favour of it. Let there be at least beers on board. So long, fellas, cheers for now. See you tomorrow.

19th August 2022, Friday

There were these seven small birds, not the sea birds, but the birds from the port of TUXPAN, Mexico. Just beside the tanker terminal was the jetty of bulk carriers. The bulk carriers have holds to carry grain mostly. So, during loading and unloading, some grain does get littered in the port, feeding thousands of small and big hungry birds. From my port hole, I used to see pigeons and hawks (feeding on pigeons), small sparrows and some seagulls daily hovering around the bulky jetty. Also, a few would stray and land on our vessel, the tanker. Just when we were leaving then, seven small, black-feathered birds, the size of a common sparrow, landed on our ship. Before they realised, the vessel undocked, and they came along with the ship. It's not uncommon for such birds to sail along ships and reach foreign ports. Now one of them banged straight into the wheelhouse window and died. The rest are still sleeping and waking up with the ship's crew. They live on the main deck below the pipelines. God knows who is feeding them. They are clearly not big enough to hunt, mostly living off food waste from the galley that too is covered nowadays. Luckily it rained often, so maybe water for them. Else on deck, it's only rust flakes and paints. But God looks after all.

21st August 2022, Sunday

Of the small birds, I see only three of them now. Hope they make it to port and fly off safely there, where they get food and shelter. Hope they acclimatize there. Maybe they will start a new generation of birds, whom they will father there. The first, like many migrants, to the land of hope and dreams, the USA. The week has passed here and no news of cargo yet. In hope, we keep drifting all the time. The engines are used seldom. The ship's swimming pool has started witnessing action again. I swam for an hour, after playing table tennis for another hour. The biggest challenge on board is to maintain sanity. And for that, you got to have a routine here. Evenings are pleasant, due to sunsets, especially on weekends, when most of the crew is either off or on lighter duties. On Sundays when the Indian crew is there, we have mandatory biryanis. Many of us count our days by the number of biryanis left. For me, the contract is over. I am relieved and on bonus biryanis now. I am eagerly hoping to have the last of Sunday biryanis and fly back to India, in Gurugram, near Delhi, though I am a born and brought up product of Rohtak, a district in Haryana. It is also fondly called the Texas of Haryana, India. It started in Indian Military training, where Rohtakis are called Texans.

And here I am, drifting about two hundred nautical miles, to make it to the original Texas, to Houston, maybe in the coming week. COVID cases rise and fall, but stay and don't perish. It looks like a disease to stay. A new disease was born in the years

2019 and 2020. Despite so many vaccines and real immunity caused in patients, this has so far failed to deter its coming back again and again. Many by now have had it multiple times. There was a cyclone last night, and the vessel rolled a bit due to it at night, though we had got an early warning and the captain had moved to the safer area too. In my new cabin, my luggage lies half-opened in my suitcase. There is not much news about the new British prime minister-elect after Boris Johnson, the guy with ruffled, uncombed, unkempt hair. The UK is planning to return some artifacts from its museum back to India. They must have brought those during Raj days in India. The UK is no longer an Empire. The only thing that they have to flaunt is the Commonwealth Games, perhaps. The Scots also want an out. England and Wales is perhaps all that the UK is now. But the UK has opened up like the USA. This might help them resurge back to glory. Post Russo-Ukraine war, equations will change in Europe – East and West Europe, that is. India always will remain a neutral terrain for sure.

22nd August 2022, Monday

The birds were not seen today, none of them. We get orders now for the vessel, to load in Pasadena and to discharge that cargo in Manaus, Brazil. We would load gasoline, high sulphur diesel, and low sulphur diesel in Pasadena. It would be a fourteen-day voyage to Manaus, upriver in Amazon. It's a three to four-day pilotage in the river. Both banks of the river have Amazon forests. I have been there before. At the night you hear crickets chirping and see the fireflies glow, and the ship sails at low speed under the local pilot's guidance. So, I will not go there, and instead I will head back home and eagerly await my tickets. The repairs on the No. 3 unit of the main engine are now imminent, and they shall be carried on at outer anchorage, near Houston. We are now underway, steaming towards that. The vessel has a lay can period from 26th August to 28th August. We will do major unit work on the 24th, to finish the same in fourteen to eighteen hours. The vessel shall tender NOR then at one a.m. on 26th August and we will go inside the port to load. Tomorrow, I shall look for little birdies. I was hoping they would make it to port. I hope they were hiding somewhere on deck. Tomorrow day will also be utilized to prepare a new liner, new piston, and other spares to renew on the 24th a.m. hours. I shall be back.

23rd August 2022, Tuesday

I walked around the ship's poop deck, around the accommodation on the upper deck, and the garbage area behind it. On the main deck, the forecastle deck. Looked beneath piping and around tank tops. In the save all trays. The remaining three birds, the little ones, were nowhere to be found. They are gone now, forever. They lost their way, lost their lives too. The ship has now anchored herself at outer anchorage off Houston. Other lives than those of humans are way too cheap. Tomorrow, we are replacing the liner and piston with new piston rings. Already, by four p.m., the cylinder head of the No. 3 unit is out. The ship will be without her engines, likely till six p.m. tomorrow or later. So, we are now perched on mud, with anchor flukes sunk in it and that's all. If the vessel drags anchor, it could be catastrophic as to it may run aground and or hit other vessels at anchorage or in harbour. As the proximity to port or other vessels is very near, as low as five cables of length. Tomorrow or the day after, we may have firm orders post-repairs to berth at Kinder Morgan berth in Pasadena. Guys have already sighted shopping malls, strip joints, etc. on the net about six miles closer to Kinder Morgan berth. I had shore leave only once, in Amsterdam, in the last one hundred and forty days. Men look forward to shore leaves.

24th August 2022, Wednesday

Unit No. 3 of the main engine was decarbonized, and a major overhaul concluded. The day began at six a.m. and we very well concluded the job by six p.m., ending with the trying out and testing of the main engine. Those unit overhaul tasks are gruelling. Despite me being not in charge, I donned my boiler suit and safety shoes, gloves, etc., and pitched in with my help. With limited breaks and precision work required, it was a tiresome job. Old liner pulled out; old piston pulled out. Now one takes their place in the engine frame, with all new 'O' rings and gaskets too. Finally, when the jacket water and lube oil, fuel oil connection was done and tested by opening valves and raising the required temperatures, all heard a sign of relief. The lemon water was a welcome break in between. During my customary evening walk, I was greeted by eight or nine seagulls calling in tandem, as if they mourned the little sea birdies' loss. Life on board is very lonely. The birds, the sound of sea waves, the rain, etc. are welcome breaks. Most retire in their cabins with something on their computer, as if to forget they are not at sea. COVID has brought severe restrictions when in ports. But luckily the USA has shore leaves to offer to tired sailors. Thank you, the USA, for that; others should follow suit. Ukraine and Russia are still at war. Not much news of monkeypox now. Hope it dies down and does not become yet another pandemic. I am now eagerly waiting for my tickets – so are three more crew on board. Apart from salaries, we don't have much left now on merchant ships. But poverty brings us back into sailings at sea.

25th August 2022, Thursday

There were some links broken in the anchor chain. An ashore-based team was hired to repair the same. Repairs were carried out on both anchors. The anchor was heaved and lowered directly into the boat, and welders fixed the parted welding of the studs. The garbage was off-landed onto the same boat. Two hundred mt of water, too, is being loaded, which started at six p.m. and will go on up to four a.m. of 26th. Tomorrow, service boats are expected to come with technicians and spares. A hydro blaster is coming to upgrade the deck, by removing the surface layer on the deck at about seven hundred bars of hydro pressure and then painting. After surface preparation, a specialist Ukrainian crew will join the vessel and sail from Houston till maybe Manaus. There is news of two ABs and a messman coming to relieve hands on board. They will be coming from the Philippines, and the off-signers will go to India. No news of berthing for the ship and hence no news of my ticket too. Guys are looking towards a voyage to Brazil. The embargo on alcohol may be lifted in September, that's good news here. The crew is hoping for a shore leave in Brazil too, where there is more action in nightlife compared to daytime shopping in US malls. Sailors always know the best hangouts all around the world. The shore leaves are important to break the mundane and vicious cycle of work, eating, and sleep patterns at sea. My luggage is open and scattered; the moment I have news I will pack my bags and merrily leave the ship, for stepping on land.

26th August 2022, Friday

The provisions, ration, and stores. Spares for machines were picked up today from the boat Mary D. The news has reached the ship that there will be no crew change. So, the bosun, a fitter who is perhaps unaware that he would go, an AB, another AB (unplanned), the GS are all disappointed. The CDC holds no meaning nowadays. To sign off in the USA, bosun and fitter didn't have a US visa, but the rest had it. So, it is likely that a reliever will not be travelling from the Philippines to relieve them. The men are, will be, shattered, they don't know it yet. For me, I continue to be in limbo, as there is no talk of me going either, though my reliever on board for the last twenty days, since TUXPAN, Mexico. Vessel berthing prospects are not known as yet. Such is life on board, changing every hour. Getting off ships is a nightmare now for sailors. Many countries simply don't allow it. Many have stringent rules and regulations. Owners and operations focus merely on budgets. Men are like sheep, herded, shorn off their wool, and disposed of at will and convenience of the person who was to sign off. Some have run into their tenth month or so. Some have not yet completed the contract. I have a reliever on board, but so far none getting down. My news might be only clear in a day or two. From my port hole, I see a distant city, only its lights and skyline visible. About fifty ships are anchored, waiting for their turns to load, repair, and move on.

27th August 2022, Saturday

Twists and turns. As I said, life on board is never static, but dynamic. Now, after rigorous pressure from off-signers, and solid pursuance from Capt. Menon, the company has relented to let the on-signers come to Houston and let crew with valid visas (US) to off-sign, and I shall leave too now along with them. The on-signers will arrive on the 29th. We will leave the vessel, subject to going alongside berth and our tickets arriving to us then. A sigh of relief was heaved by all concerned. The quality of water at the outer anchorage is not all that great. We tried to go for a swim in the vessel's pool, but it was muddy and not clear. So midway stopped the fun. Now those who will sail will do so on the high seas, in clear blue water. What a stress buster that small pool is. It is a social hangout, too. Back home in India, vaccines for COVID go on, and on. Now, booster doses have begun for the second dose. In the US Open, Djokovic again was dropped due to not being allowed entry by US authorities, same as in the Australian Open, as he is not vaccinated. Anyway, God knows if these vaccines are effective. Almost all those who have had vaccines have contracted COVID once or multiple times. Tomorrow in India, there is a Pak cricket T20 match and that's something to look forward to in the weekend on board. Tomorrow is Sunday, a relatively easy day at ship.

28th August 2022, Sunday

So, the Sunday biryani is done. And Sunday, the day is gone. It's the night of Sunday. Yes, there is yet no news of vessel berthing. The two on-signers have probably already flown from the Philippines and would land in Houston by tomorrow. We are yet awaiting our tickets home. Waiting is tiresome; it's more tiring than rigorous vessel jobs. I am now particularly detached, as I have been relieved of my duties too. The shoreline is lit up at night. Shore certainly calms a sailor, merely the sight does. My writing accounts of these days are to let people in present and in the future know of two things. That there is a pandemic, and how seafarers have dealt with it. And how the world ignored seafarers too. The whole world's supply chains were never cut off. Not even in the peak of corona days. Not in 2019, not in 2020, not in 2021, not in 2022. And we tirelessly go on. When the world was totally shut, we kept joining ships and kept serving chartered flights that took us to seas. And we kept ships going from one country to another, moving medicines, oil, food, grains, clothes, and all that is used by modern day. We are not allowed to go out to shore leaves in most cities, even now. And in the peak, sailors were locked in ships for as long as a year and more, often running out of water and food. What keeps us going is our duties towards families first, and then honestly towards our job profiles. One day people might notice how we are connecting dots in the world.

29th August 2022, Monday

There is finally a talk about my tickets. It might be the 31st of August or the 1st of September that I may fly. The ship may berth on 31st Aug or 1st September. The ships keep sailing, newer sailors keep coming. There will be tides at sea. Full moons and sunrises. Ships will keep going on high seas and touching foreign shores. Men like me will keep coming to write, to try to tell the tales at sea, of sea, of ships. But a pen cannot really sum up either the glory of the sea or the miracle of how a ship sails and survives. Or how a sailor braves it. It can only be felt by one at sea on a seagoing duty. Not many know, not many tell, that from their first ships, sailors wish that it's their last, but they keep coming. In Europe, earlier Church fathers would come to bless sailors. Schoolchildren will bring clothes, needles, threads, and books for sailors. I was once told that sailors are damned, so they come to sea. But sea pursues them too; it's like purgatory. It cleanses you and heals you too. It toughens you up too, like forging steel. I once read, "If someone does not believe in God send him for sailing." Out at sea, you realize how trivial a man is, and how powerful nature is. Rumor has it now that many countries like India, Australia, and Canada have passed orders to offer compulsory shore leaves to seafarers, which means they cannot be denied if they wish to step ashore. God bless them. The on-signers have passed the mandatory RTPCR test and are fit to join. The off-signers will go by the airline's requirements of COVID protocol. India defeated arch-rivals Pak in the cricket T20 yesterday.

30th August 2022, Tuesday

I have my tickets now from Houston to Istanbul, to Delhi, via Turkish airlines. A sixteen-and-a-half-hour flight from Houston to Istanbul and a six-hour flight from Istanbul to Delhi. It will be almost six hours from the ship via boat to the airport after all mandatory clearances. The boat will come to take us. Along with me also go the GS, Rao, and AB, Anil Kumar. Their relievers will come in the same boat that we will leave on. I love sign offs by the boats, rather than from the piers via taxi. You can see your ship fading away slowly when the boat keeps moving away farther. The ship now has the schedule. She will berth on the evening of the 2nd. But I will be gone by then, in Istanbul. I will reach Delhi at four-forty a.m. on the the TK 716, last flight to Delhi. This might be my last ship. But that I say leaving all my ships. Time only will tell. She is called Hafnia Phoenix, under command of Capt. Menon. Chief Engineer, Parminder Singh. Second Engineer, Praveen Sawant. Third Engineer, Ankit Negi. Electrical officer, Shizo. Fourth Engineer, Siva. Second officer, Swapnil. Chief officer, Ajinkja. Third officer, Kiran Pal. It's sad. I will forget the names of the men I sailed with one day. But then, it's been twenty-six years and a greater number of ships than years. Roughly, I have sailed with about five hundred men during my time. So far, I am thankful to all of them for their cooperation, help, and memories. You all were my family at sea.

31st August 2022, Wednesday

The story every day at sea is full of twists and turns. My ticket got cancelled. Now new issues, which are Houston to Chicago to Delhi. Supposedly, a not so liked or preferred airline and American carrier. Turkish Airlines is gone, which I could have preferred due to the long haul. Anyways, now the scene is that the boat with spares and stores will reach Hafnia Phoenix tomorrow post noon. If that reaches, it will bring along two new on-joiners from the Philippines, the AB and the GS. Whether the off-signer AB and GS and I will go back to Houston on the same launch is not yet confirmed. If not, we might stay on the vessel, considering she berths on 2nd Sept. If so, we will go on that boat and on that flight. But it appears now that days are numbered now on this Ship. This might be the last night of mine on this tour of duty. This might even be the last night of my sailing days as a regular chief engineer of merchant ships and that of a ship's regular crew. I might not be back, or I may as an auditor or inspector, maybe still in the same role. That only time will tell. But am keen on leaving after an energy-sapping twenty-six years of my youth dedicated to seagoing duties on ships. I have memories galore and they rush by at times. The days and nights in Brazilian clubs, or days of Italian ports. Shore leaves by launches, lazy strolls by beaches, and drunk passing out while coming back during the good old days. Now it's a new world, and I often feel like an outsider now.

1st September 2022, Thursday

Every hour, the dynamics change on board. Now the Houston-Chicago-Delhi flight of United American Airlines stands cancelled, as the rule says, and outbound travellers from the ship must straight away depart from the USA and cannot go to another city. And also, must fly away before the ship departs port. So much of a burden to be a developed numero uno country. I think this is perhaps so that poor seafarers do not jump ship and run away into their fairyland. America is also one of, if not the numero uno in obesity. Perhaps riches bring out laziness and pride. Now, a new ticket that has been issued will fly me to Houston, Doha, and Delhi. If this goes through, I leave the vessel by post-noon hours. The ship was piloted today and brought into the harbour and port. Now, it is moored alongside the jetty. There are lights galore all around in the port area, almost like a Diwali here. A dredger is merrily dredging the silt near our vessel. Houston certainly is one of the busiest ports in the world. While making port, I saw gas carriers, containers, general cargo, tankers towed barges, and all sorts of vessels. Almost all the piers along the way are busy loading and unloading ships. Although, the backwaters are dark, filthy, and have lots of floats on top. The banks are dirty too. There is almost no aesthetic sense. Only money-making machines are all around. Europe is prettier that way. My bags are still unpacked; maybe tomorrow I will pack and leave the ship.

5th September 2022, Monday

Finally home now, when I am writing this piece. A sought-after Qatar Airways flight took me home. The flight from George Bush International Houston was late for almost two and a half hours, and this made us miss the next flight from Doha to Delhi so we had to catch another rescheduled flight. But home now. Thus, the day's write-up is dedicated to Sheikh Tamim Bin Hamad Al Thani, Son of Hamad Bin Khalifa, after whose name the famous, glorious Doha Hamad International airport is named. Thank you, King Tamim Bin Hamad Al Thani Ji, for the mariner's exclusive lounge that you have made for sailors. It's so fabulous, so well kept, and so much in taste with times. World-class coffee machines with freshly roasted coffee beans used, the shower, and the lavatories were all so thoughtful and of so much use to us sailors. Sir, thank you from me, from the entirety of the seamen who were there, when we clapped for your generosity, with loud applause. On 3rd September 2022, Saturday, 12:13 a.m. local time, Fourth Officer Nhilfe Linao took pictures of us, me, GS Rao, AB Anil, Third Officer Jerry Alanao and so many more were there. We all thank you, Sheikh Saheb. No one but you cared about us, thousands of vagabonds, homeless, and ship workers. May Allah bless you with eternal peace, happiness, and wealth that knows no bounds. Thank you, sir.

9th September 2022, Friday

Queen of queens and kings and that of presidents, prime ministers, and of nations. The one perhaps and the only one ever, the longest reigning monarch, the ruler of an erstwhile world, which was under her forefathers', fore-kings and queens, command. A ruler of seventy-two years as Queen of England and the UK and the British Empire that was Queen Elizabeth is no more. She peacefully passed over. And Charles now becomes the King at seventy-three years. Ninety-six-year-old Queen Elizabeth now has gone into another world. She passed away at Balmoral Castle in Scotland. I wish her a well-deserved rest in another world. God knows when the world will hear now "Long live the Queen". Charles will now be an automatic monarch. His coronation may take some time, though we now live in a much more open world. My daughter, Varalika, is a few days away from going to London for her Master's in Law at the prestigious King's College. I and many from my generation and most of the next generation of mine are no longer racist, religious fanatics. Even the world's boundaries do not deter our love for other lands. The aftereffects of corona are now seen in the populace, which are breathlessness, palpitations of the heart, headaches, fever, joint pains, and neuro diseases. Most almost one hundred per cent of my contacts have been COVID positive now. During my entire coming back journey from the ship, there were no precautions, checks, or tests for COVID on passengers. The world has come to terms with this pandemic. A new disease is now already born.

It will recur and get cured; a better line of treatment will emerge. The trigger when I started writing this book was the COVID, but I drifted onto daily news worldwide. It is an account of my views on the world in 2019, 2020, 2021, and 2022. My travels, travails, my sailings, my personal happiness, my losses, like each one out there. I lost my father, and my daughter completed LLB and is going for her Master's in Law. I have seen a sea change in the world in these years. These were really changing times. The world's health, economy, the equations all changed. I wrote the anecdotes for future readers. The current readers can read and keep their copies for their children to know a simple account of these years. It's the rainy season now in North India, but minus the rains. In summers in England, streets tar melted at forty degrees Celsius. The world over, the weather has changed. Rishi Sunak lost his bid to be UK PM. The UK, I think, is not yet as fully Cosmopolitan as the USA. The future surely will belong to Cosmo citizens of the world.

"Vasudhaiv Kutumbkam"-Whole world is my family.

15th October 2022, Saturday

My ink starts to dry now in the pen. COVID is leaving, almost leaving the world. Unless its venomous head springs any surprise. I hope not. The cases have dropped to minimal levels and are on the way out from the pandemic in the world.

Russia continues to pound Ukraine, but I hope it ceases as the disease is leaving too. People have learned to live with COVID. Doctors have learned to treat and cure. Scientists have vaccines against it now.

We saw a disease being born and a cure emerging. The hope has won again. The world has crawled back to normalcy. The passenger ships, hotels, and resorts are back, along with smiles on their faces.

May all who were lost to corona attain peace. For some unknown reasons, I have always loved and cherished Queen Elizabeth, and have waited to see the Crown shift to the new King Charles. An era comes to an end with the passing away of Queen. An era begins with the coronation of the new king of the UK. *These were melancholy times of...*

"Queen, Corona, Coronation."